COSMIC FLASHES

By
Sri Swami Omkar

Edited by
Prof. S.P. Ruhela

Regency Publications
New Delhi

By the same author

COSMIC FAST
IN THE HOURS OF SILENCE
CONTROL OF MIND
GOD REALISATION NOW AND HERE
OM JAPA
SOHAM etc., etc.

First Edition 1953
Second Editon 1959
Third Editon 1998

ISBN 81-86030-73-5

Published by Regency Publications, 20/36-G, Old Market, West Patel Nagar, New Delhi 110 008, India and printed at Radiant Printers, New Delhi 110 008, Phones: 574 0038, 571 2539; Telefax: 578 3571.

May the *Cosmic Flashes*
bless you with Cosmic Light
is the prayer of your brother

Omkar

Inhale and Exhale Peace — Thy Birthright

TRUTH IS ONE, MEN CALL IT VARIOUSLY

O Brother man, fold to thy heart thy brother!
Where pity dwells, the joy of peace is there;
To worship rightly is to love each other,
Each smile hymn, each kindly deed prayer.

FOREWORD TO FIRST EDITION

My thanks are due to Sri. K. Satchidanandamurty, the distinguished author and thinker, for his learned Introduction of this book. I am afraid that he has written much in appreciation of the 'COSMIC FLASHES' merely out of his great love for me. For my part I shall feel that labour in writing these thoughts is not wasted if my loving readers should read and assimilate the essence of at least one simple thought out of these 108 messages and derive benefit therefrom.

As temperaments of people vary, all the messages may not be appealing to all the readers but I feel confident that everyone will find some message or other practical and helpful and that which touches his or her own heart. These simple messages may not be appealing to the intellectuals and professors. And *Jivanmuktas* — the Liberated-in-life, do not need any messages from anyone.

As a boy I read in the Bible that the Holy Christ fasted for Forty Days in the wilderness. As I read it, I too longed to fast sometime like the Blessed Christ for forty days. By His Grace my simple desire was fulfilled by this fast of forty days in the wilderness of Totapalli Hills.

Before sending these Cosmic Flashes to the Press, I had the joy of reading them to myself one morning in Kailas, with the wide ocean on one side and the blue hills on the other. The messages filled me with feelings of ecstasy that I cannot describe. As I came to the last chapter, the One Hundred and Eighth, which was concluded with a small poem on Somebody, I longed to be that Somebody to my loving Readers of these Cosmic Flashes. Beloved Readers, may I have that blessed privilege of serving you in Silence from Kailas!

As the wise and aspiring do not need more words, I leave you now in SILENCE to allow the Cosmic Flashes to pervade and permeate the very cells of your beings.

May Peace be unto all!
OM TAT SAT OM!

Mt. Kailas
Waltair
1st Sept. 1953

Swami Omkar

EDITOR'S NOTE

Swami Omkar of Sri Santi Ashram, East Godavari District, Andhra Pradesh was a great Harbinger of Peace in this Century. All his life he pioneered the cause of Universal Peace. His PEACE PRAYER is the most illuminating and soothing prayer which spreads waves of Peace all over the universe. Since the greatest need of the world throughout this Century has been Peace and in future also this would be the greatest need, we must earnestly appreciate the relentless and remarkable efforts of this great Spiritual Master of our Age.

This book '*Cosmic Flashes*' was authored by Swami Omkar during a long fast for 40 days in March-April 1950. He had wished it to be read, understood, discussed and freely re-published, presented and enjoyed by all those who stand committed to the concept of Universal Peace.

Sri. A. Somasundaram, Founder & Honorary Secretary of Divine Centre, Markapur, whom I consider as my '*Spiritual Father*' was privileged to be in constant communion with the great Saint Swami Omkar for several decades. In June 1997 he developed in me great reverence and attraction for Swami Omkar, and gave me this book for reprinting after due editing.

I have therefore edited it, and included some useful material and a valuable write-up on 'The Philosophy of Swami Omkar' in it to make it all the more useful.

Grateful thanks are due to revered Swami Omkar, and Sri A. Somasundaramji.

This book is dedicated to the memory of this Great Apostle of Peace and to all those who wish to work as dedicated spiritual soldiers committed to win Peace for all the creatures of this world.

June 16, 1998

Dr. S.P. Ruhela
Sai Divine Research Centre
126, Sector 37, Faridabad 121003

INTRODUCTION

The following pages were written by Sri Swami Omkar in 1950 during a fast which lasted for forty days.

Swami Omkar is a mystic. I do not now wish to discuss the value and validity of mystic consciousness. But I must point out that Swami Omkar's mysticism is virile and rationalistic — to the extent mysticism could be rationalistic. He does not claim to have had any peculiar visions or weird dreams. He, of course, has realized the unity of the whole world in the one thing Real — the Spirit. He has no attachment of any sort to dogmas and creeds, nor is his love and friendship limited to one country or nation. His is a global view — a view which embraces Man as such. In like way he worships God — not the God revealed in this religion or that — but God who is claimed to be revealed in every religion, but who is fully and perfectly revealed in none.

Obviously those who are imprisoned within their own parochial grooves mistake him. The Jews of his day excommunicated Spinoza. And when Hegelian theologians like Troeltsch declared that Christianity is not the absolute religion, critics were not wanting. I am sure followers of other religions also would react in the same way, if they are told that their scriptures too do not contain the last word of wisdom. This is inevitable. If one wants to rally a following and command an influence, he must take shelter under a banner, adopt a slogan and then sound the drum. Brave as he is to the core, Swami Omkar refuses to become a slave of anybody or any "ism". He stands by himself and that only in Truth for him, which he has discovered or which he has assimilated. He is literally *atmani sthithah* (established in Atman). It is for this I admire him and it is this in his admirable personality that has attracted me.

I have been intimate with many religious men both Christian and Hindu. But no where do I find freedom from servility to a particular tradition and dogma. It is all right if one has entered into the tradition — whether it is Biblical or Vedic — and understood and appropriated the truth it contains. But that is lacking. Often one adopts *Advaita* because Sankara taught it and one hails Realism because Saint Aquinas advocated it. But have we no duty to understand and rationally assimilate what Sankara and Aquinas said and ought we not reject whatever refuses to be rationally assimilated? Intellectual integrity, I am sure, must have a place everywhere, including religion. In Swami Omkar I find this.

Many in India and overseas know Swami Omkar. He has extensively travelled in Europe and America. His Ashramas at Totapalli (East Godavari) and Waltair (Visakhapatnam) are famous. For over three decades his Ashrama has toiled for the spread of the concepts of Human brotherhood and Peace among all nations. Through talks and writings, through pamphlets and journals he has done this. Some branches of his Ashram have been opened on the other side of the Atlantic and also in the land of Goethe and Hegel. All this is good but the results are not spectacular. That is as it must be; for the labourers are few and the vineyard is so unwieldy and weedy.

And now about this book: I must say I find it wonderful. Made up of one hundred and eight chapters, it presents to us as many meditations. It is something like Pascal's 'Pensees'. No doubt we miss that splendid literary elegance and also that razor-edged keenness of the great Frenchman. But can that Jansenist Catholic thinker claim as much width and as much real catholicity as Sri Swami Omkar shows in this brief but memorable book?

I aver that the following pages are full of sustaining inspiration and deep meaning.

Prof. K. Satchidanandamurty
Dept. of Philosophy, Andhra University
Waltair

that Jansenist Catholic thinker contains as much wisdom and as much real catholicity as Sri Swami Omkar shows in this brief but memorable book?

I aver that the following pages are full of sustaining inspiration and deep meaning.

Prof. K. Satchidananda Murty
Dept. of Philosophy, Andhra University,
Waltair

CONTENTS

SECTION I

NAMELESS REALM OF BLISS

Your Peace is My Peace

May I have the privilege of serving you to help yourself to establish PEACE in your heart and radiate IT in your home converting it into a HEAVEN OF PEACE.

May you express PEACE in thought, word and deed thus help to vibrate IT from heart to heart, in the Community, Nation and the World at large, until PEACE pervades and permeates the Whole Universe, through your IDEAL LIFE OF PEACE. This is the prayer of your OMKAR.

OM! OM! OM!

When you can see the ONE in the many, you are always alone with ME. Then nothing else can exist besides ME — the one without a second. God fulfils all sacred dreams and right desires sooner or later. The buds bloom only in their appointed time or season. Unnatural anxiety or hurry over them, does not hasten or help the full bloom of flowers; neither the fulfilment of our ambitions and undertakings.

Let Sun Beams burst from our loving hearts ceaselessly until they fill and refill the whole world creating one luminous man of stupendous light of the SUN of SUNS.

Bless me with the life of a sweet smelling fragrant flower. This life too is only temporary and evanescent. Instead of living like a Banayan tree or an oak tree for a thousand years, better to live a life of fragrance, beauty and service even if it is for a day and then to pass on to higher realms.

When one identifies himself with the SPIRIT — the Indwelling presence — all days are alike.

As I may never get this blessed opportunity again, let me not waste even an hour or a minute in vain, but make the best use of every moment in reaching higher and thus coming nearer to Thee day by day. This is all I pray of Thee.

Whenever my eyes wandered towards His picture, I conversed with HIM trying to feel His tender love and spirit and await an answer. But He neither spoke nor smiled but continued to look into my heart and soul with His penetrating eyes of love as if asking me to MERGE within to be still and to listen to His answer in the stillness of my heart.

FASTING and SILENCE are the imperishable mines of wealth for all seekers of peace. If there is anything most pathetic in this world, it is to see the sad and helpless state of a man who is a slave of the senses, restlessly suffering day and night with numberless desires. His desires will not allow him either to rest or to sleep. Desire alone is the root cause of all physical and mental diseases. It is wonderful to desire the highest. I AM WITH YOU. The conception of God and of His existence varies according to the state and stage of the individual evolution. May I request you to meditate with me for a little while feeling His presence forgetting all else at least for the time being.

Very soon I felt overshadowed by the consciousness of a lovely sacred presence enfolding me as a Zephyr enfolds a drowsy, closed flower at even-tide. The heavenly dew, tears of ecstasy, began to flow from my eyes. There is no end to activities in the Ashram or the world. It resembles a cascade of water ever tumbling down, with always more to come. But what a happy thought, so is also the boundless love of God a perennial flow of the living water of life —

LIGHT AND LOVE. The more we delight in it, the more HIS spirit outpours upon and through us.

It is resolved in memory of this sacred fast to weed out these three latent impressions from my life — worry, fear and expectation. Worry leads one nowhere but to decay and old age fear saps our life's blood leading us to an early grave. Expectation kills the present moment of peace and joy leading to false hopes and empty delusions regarding the future. As we think so we become, we reap what we sow and thoughts are things. It has been said that man is a bundle of impressions, thought — impressions that are the result of desires. Desires are the outcome of attachment to objects of the world, be they good or bad. We are all slaves of our own habits in some form or the other. Work done in the right spirit, and with proper understanding exhilarates the spirit, strengthens the mind and stimulates the soul and body. Hence it has been quoted that those who have found their real life-work are indeed blessed.

MEN of GOD-realisation say that the perennial spring of Amrita is ceaselessly flowing in every one of us and those who are selfless and God-imbued can drink it. Such lives are a blessings unto all. God is certainly with me ceaselessly watching, protecting and blessing me with His love and Divine strength. FORGETFULNESS OF GOD IS DEATH. DO NOT LOVE BUT LIVE AS LOVE.

I need Thee; My Lord, I need Thee always. I need Thee more than ever now. Without Thee I cannot live any longer. We are filled with and surrounded on everyside by His love and this is at all times. I often emphasise what we need for our emancipation or freedom is recognition and awareness. I am in the heart of God. We are rich or poor, young or old, healthy or sick, virtuous or sinful but we are all in the Heart of God. There is never a moment when we can slip out of

HIS UNIVERSAL HEART. This one fact or truth is enough for our SALVATION.

When the body is pure, the mind is also pure and when the mind is pure, the self or God manifests in the mirror of one's own soul. So long as Moon of love and wisdom does not shine in our lives, they are veiled in darkness. When once the Radiant truth begins to shine within oneself, slowly its light spreads everywhere and radiates all over the world like the light of an ascending moon in a clear blue sky.

I awakened early from a pleasant dream, feeling a mystic joy and inspiration. It is in STILLNESS in the deep stillness that can be compared to the quiet ocean depths that we realise God. So we have been taught in Bible "BE STILL AND KNOW THAT I AM GOD." OMNIPOTENCE is working, let the mortal retire "SAMADHI" NIRVANA. Nectar of immortality, Kingdom of Heaven or Peace that passeth all understanding, will be the immediate and direct result, only when the mortals retire completely and not until then.

NATIONAL CODE OF CONDUCT FOR THE CITIZENS OF INDIA

1. PATRIOTISM: Our Motherland should be our first and highest consideration. Welfare of the nation is our own welfare. Therefore, let us willingly be ready to offer up even our own life for our country. Let us inculcate in our children and members of our family love for our country, the spirit of patriotism and service of our country and our fellow citizens.
2. DUTY: Our first and foremost duty is to God and to Righteousness. Leading a righteous life is the best and most valuable service of our Nation.
3. CHARACTER: Character is the greatest wealth. A pure, incorruptible citizen is the greatest asset of our Nation. This is vital and indispensable. Therefore, good character is to be given top priority value; upon this depends our nation's welfare and its future stability.
4. HEALTH: Health is the basis of success. Health is wealth. Next to character, it is the greatest national asset. As citizens, building up character and safeguarding health, should be our primary duty to the Nation.
5. VIRTUE: Let us join hands and eradicate the evils of gambling, liquor-drinking, drug-taking, tobacco-smoking and betel-chewing. Let us eradicate the evils of bribery, corruption, selfishness, immorality, dishonesty and mis-

conduct. Disloyalty to our Nation is crime and unpardonable sin.

6. PUBLIC PROPERTY: O Citizen! We are the custodian of public property. Let us not spoil, misuse, steal or destroy National property. Let us keep our country neat and clean. This is your sacred duty.
7. ONE FAMILY: All our citizens are brethren. Let us feel this fraternity. Let us love each other and one another and be united, because we are one family.
8. RELIGION: We must have equal reverence for all religions, creeds and faiths. Let us love as our own brothers the followers of all our faiths. Let us treat others as we wish to be treated by them.
9. NON-VIOLENCE: At all costs avoid every type of violence and hatred, for this is a blot on the fair name of the Nation. It is soul-killing and causing great harm to our country's welfare and development, It is totally opposed to our Nation's ideal.
10. ECONOMY: Let us adopt simple living and high thinking. Let us not be extravagant. Let us avoid waste. Let us practise frugality. Let us share what we have with our less fortunate fellow citizens. This is National virtue that our India needs today.
11. LAW: Let us respect the rule of law and uphold social justice. In this lies the guarantee of our welfare and orderly progress towards better India.
12. AHIMSA: Non-injury is our highest virtue (*Ahimsa Paramo Dharmah*). Compassion is a divine quality. Protection of animals is our sacred duty. This is India's special teaching. Let us be compassionate towards all creatures. Thus be a true Indian. Try to become an embodiment of kindness compassion and goodness in your every day life.

13. ECOLOGY: Man and Nature are inseparable, Man and his natural environment are inter-related and mutually interdependent. Everything in Nature contributes to our protection and nourishment. Let us, therefore, protect our natural environment. Helping in maintaining the ecological balance is our duty. It is indispensable for our safe living and highest welfare. Polluting of public places and polluting of air and water of the country is a national crime. We must make amends for our past lapses.
14. UNITY: The more united the people of a country, the greater is their ability to withstand all obstacles and dangers. United we stand, divided we fall. This is particularly true about today's India. Therefore, let us live in close harmony and loving goodwill with all our countrymen. Love for our country means love for our countrymen. This is the most invaluable service a citizen of India, can offer to our Motherland.
15. EDUCATION: The process of education should incorporate within it the imparting of the basic knowledge of India's great culture, its lofty ideals and noble values and principles of living. Our education has to be oriented towards enriching and enhancing the quality of life of our youth and students.

THUS, SHINE AS A TRUE CITIZEN AND SERVE YOUR COUNTRY BEST, BY THE VERY MANNER OF YOUR LIFE AND CONDUCT.

SWAMI OMKAR
LOVER OF THE COUNTRY

THE SPIRITUAL PHILOSOPHY OF SRI SWAMI OMKAR

A. Somasundarm

I

The dictionary meaning of the word 'Philosophy' is, the knowledge of causes of Phenomena of both mind and matter. In the medieval ages, it was used for pursuit of knowledge and it included all branches of learning. It is, therefore, when a university gives a degree of doctorate, it does not necessarily mean proficency in mental and moral philosophy such as psychology, meta-physics, ethics etc; but any branch of learning. Literally, however the word Philosophy does not include physical science or liberal arts. More or less it is spoken for metaphysics.

Who is a philosopher? He is one who in the pursuit of knowledge gathers certain characteristics especially calmness of temper, practical wisdom and sedateness of judgment. We are concerned here with the vital subject of life's philosophy. When we explain any phenomenon or device, that method of explanation is called philosophy. Similarly, life has its philosophy and that philosophy is the most enthralling and enticing of all for it deals with the most vital questions concerning man and for that reason it is of supreme importance. We generally consider the visible as real. But really speaking what is invisible is the real and not the visible. God is really unknowable and incomprehensible, when we use the telescope of reason to discern Him, but to the eye of mystic, to one who has deep and abiding love and devotion to God, He is not a veiled identity or an unknown and unknowable being. It has been man's search throughout the corridor of time, to unveil the secrets of nature and to discover the Primordial source of all existence. The hunger for search is innate in man.

No man can live without philosophy. Each one has to be a philosopher in the right sense of the word. There have been various systems of philosophy adumbrated from time to time. Every religion has its philosophy and a deep study of all religions of the world not only indicates the true purpose of life but gives ample food for spiritual unfoldment to understand and comprehend the ultimate Reality — God and the inexorable Laws of the universe. When Socrates said, "Virtue is Knowledge", he was giving expression to a certain truth. In the pursuit after the knowledge of God, purity of life is a sine qua non. Socrates has left an undying name because of his insistence on virtue and sacrifice. Virtue is his whole philosophy, whole knowledge. An ugly man, clad in tatters, sitting in a corner of a street, he became the target of earnest inquirers after truth. The Athenians listened to his words of wisdom with rapt attention. But he was wrongly accused of corrupting the morals of the young and he died drinking cheerfully the cup of hemlock. But Socrates lives in our hearts as a monument of virtue and sacrifice.

When one reads the life of Jesus Christ the God-Man, the village Carpenter, about his sufferings, the trials and humiliations, which the sinless man passed through, healing the lepers, preaching to the masses in the language of parables, the final trial and crucifixion and resurrection, one feels bewildered that even when such a man, the very incarnation of God, was sent to absolve the world from its sinfulness and inspite of the fact that nearly one third of the human race professes Christianity as its religion, there is so very little of it in this world. Christ's great teaching of Love is the rock and foundation of all other virtues, and above all his teachings of the ultimate aim of Life viz., union with God, forms the hallmark of his great and sublime religion.

"The man of God is the man of Peace. Rather give away your land, your house, your wife, your children than take an axe and strike it against another even in self-defence. The teaching of non-violence preached by that great soul of India, Mahatma Gandhi should infiltrate in every part and parcel of every country in the world. Non-violence is the greatest weapon that man can use even in self-defence. "Mahatma Gandhi had not died in vain. He was chosen by God to become a martyr to bring about a searching of heart among people maddened with religious fever of wrong type. Universal brotherhood combined with tolerance and liberality of thought will form the chief feature of the new age which will shortly follow." (Rishi Ram Ram).

I have given the above soul-churning tragedies of great saints to awaken human consciousness, to stir public mind to realise the value and purpose of human birth a precious gift of God — God Realise, action — and that the essence of human life is sacrifice.

It has taken over a million years for the evolution of Man — the animal man into human man. But the ancient seers or *rishis* were not satisfied with the growth of Man on the physical plane alone. They searched for and found the clues. The *rishis* were scientists of consciousness. The Word *Rishi* comes from the Sanskrit Word *RU* meaning to investigate. "The *Rishis* of India were the earliest revealers of the secrets of nature in a systematic form. They were great enlightened souls in communion with God. They gave universal teachings of deepest significance. They were the first research workers in the laboratory of Divine Mystery. They spoke only one language — the language of Truth imbibed by them direct from God" (Rishi Ram Ram).

The Rishis were more or less subjective scientists, but they left behind a message, an objective message for all of us. They looked upon their body as a Cosmic Laboratory, a vehicle to conduct cosmic experiments and not simply an apparatus of *bhoga* or sense gratification.

Remember the world is not a play boy club, but a university of learning. Nothing is free here, and each one of us must learn the lessons fully and well. If we default we shall have to come back to repeat the *karmic* cycle of life and death in the same class until we earn out promotion to a higher rung in the ladder of Evolution. "The Evolution towards Spiritual condition is the movement governed by Immutable Law and every one of you should take your place in the movement which is the fulfillment of the destiny of all beings from the inanimate kingdom to the highest angels." (Rishi Ram Ram.)

Sciences are many and man acquires power to control the physical worlds through his sciences. But man cannot live by science alone. Humanity is like a lotus looking heavenwards though the roots are in the mire of animal impulses. The great humanity begins its march heavenwards. High virtues, courage, morality and all that makes life real and worth living stand like a ladder between Earth and Heaven to humanity in its march heavenwards, and every rung of the ladder, a virtue, and stained with the foot-mark of some saint who has passed onwards. History lives in the future humanity through the beaconlights and land marks left by great heroes and saints. And women have contributed no less by their life of purity, humility and reverence.

All Laws are eternal and the Law of Karma is the most ancient, most current and the most inviolable law working in all worlds except in the Spiritual plane and binding on all beings even Gods and Angels. Ideals, good intentions, evil intentions, and the Social *Karmic* factor, all work together. Wars, famines, pestilences are as much the total result of *Karma* and they form new foundation for future result also. The human race evolves in a steady course of evolution as long as the Law is correctly understood and applied. When the human evolution halts or reverses itself and begins to traverse to degradation, the Divine will sends fresh spiritual impulses in the form of an *Avatar* or prophet or a great leader or saint inspired by Divine Wisdom. Present time is at the crossroads where humanity is pulling in one direction and the Divine will in the higher direction. The time is pregnant with great possibilities for all races and nations for quick progress — spiritual — or total destruction. A New age is in the offing.

III

It is in the above background that we will have to know what this great mystic saint, Swami Omkar had left behind when he left his mortal coil on 10th June, 1982. The life he lived, the precepts he prescribed, his predilections, his religion, his concern for the common man all this make up his philosophy.

It should be remembered at the outset that Sri Swami Omkar does not belong to any community, caste or race. He is a citizen of the Cosmos. By Cosmos I mean the visible and invisible worlds, mainfest and unmanifest. His only creed, if any, is to live in God and to see others live in Him. In the printed constitution, "The Mission of Peace, Sri Santhi Asram" on the cover page we find "*Our Ideals:*

One caste, one Religion, one God. All people in the world are our sisters and brothers. To serve and love them is our religion. To establish the Brotherhood of Humanity and the Fatherhood of God is our goal. All of us, the whole creation emanates from one God."

Having given the above thrilling and soul elevating ideal while at Waltair Asram facing the ocean, Swamiji used to give us an ideal vision for every aspiring devotee in the following lines:

"My living images of God, What is you vision? Is it universal, like that of the Ocean which is facing me? Or is your vision finite, like that of a mere bubble? Are you confined to the cage of flesh, blood and bones, thinking of stomach running after the fleeting clouds of name and fame in the mirage of the world? The scriptures teach us that the Nation or people without vision will perish although they may be rich and successful in outer civilization, in the material things of the world. India still lives because of its vision of spirituality. Any nation, if it is without the firm basis of spirituality or universal love, is bound to perish and decay, fall sooner or later. Man, the finiteman, the ignorant man inspite of his bag-fulls of talk of God's Omnipresence, Omnipotence and Omniscience, when it comes to the practical, daily life, when he is doing something wrong, then he does not believe in the existence of God, the All-knowing Interpenetrating God. Such is the thick MAYA, the dark delusion of outer life."

Having given the ideal of all humanity as one family, Swamiji has classified that there are four people in the world as under:

(a) Those who wickedly ignore the existence of God of the higher life, because they are in the state of animals, ever deriving satisfaction from the contact of senses in their sensual life.

(b) Those who complain of lack of time for realizing God. There is the seed of devotion in these souls. They need only to understand the Truth and their relationship with the same and thus strive further on and on.

(c) Those who are satisfied with outer forms of religion. These should rise from non-essentials of Religion and strive to find the perennial spring of joy and Peace within themselves.

(d) Those for whom Religion is the be all and end all, those who are living as inseparably one in the past, present and future, realizing the kingdom of Heaven within themselves.

Thus classifying the entire humanity as above, Swami Omkar further adds, "if there are people who truly deserve the name, 'Images of God,' it is only such people belonging to the fourth class who are worthy. All honour and glory be unto them. By self-examination and understanding every one should see for oneself, whether one is in the first or second or third or fourth state. The first class people should try to reach the second, the second should try to reach the third and the third should strive to attain the fourth, finally reaching the highest state of realisation. Progress is Life, stagnation is Death. (Extracted from the book: ***The Soul of Omkar***).

The above classification takes us to the all-important topic of Religion — its importance in life and Swamiji's views.

Observes Sri Swami Sivananda, "the task of religion is to make men and nations, true, just, honest, sincere and divine. Practice religion then one becomes divine."

Of all the saints we have had in this century in our land it is Sri Swami Sivanandaji — that dynamic Yogi — who had to his credit about 300 books written on spiritual topics in lucid English language to suit all tastes and temperaments. We are told that once a devotee put the following question to Swamiji.

Q. "Swamiji you have written some hundreds of books. What is the essence?"

Ans. "Serve, Love, Give, Purify, Meditate Realise, Be good, Do good, Bear insult, Bear injury."

The above question and answer is of deep significance. It reveals the problem of the common man, and the present confused state in which religion is. In today's changed conditions, if the common man is to be lifted, give him the essence of religion and ask him to practice. He will progress.

Now, we have not only several religions but in each religion there are so many churches. The Christians have different churches, the Greek, the Roman Catholic the protestant and so forth. The Hindus have their Shaivites, Vaishnavites, Shaktas and various sub-sects. The Buddhists are divided into Mahayana and Hinayana and Northern and Southern Churches. The Muslims are divided into Shias and Sunnis. How can humanity, a solid unit, be cut and divided? "The main cause of war and restlessness is the division of society into rival groups" (Rishi Ram Ram).

Intense human suffering coupled with the problem of survival had stirred the consciousness of leaders of different religions over a period of almost a decade since Kyoto-Japan Conference and they have come to realise how increasingly complex are the problems facing humanity, but it is regrettable to note that they are far away to get at the solution. Remember the naked truth that the common man as well as the modern man are dissatisfied with the present role of religions. The vagaries of outer religion and the madness of religiosity — debased religion — are leading to frustration and disgust, resulting in decrying religion as an evil and God a lie. So, the first and foremost question that faces World Religions is to define Religion and what it means? Sri Swami Omkar has solved this problem once for all when he says, "I desire to define God and religion. In the highest sense they are both one and the same. God is the source of all life, both manifest and unmanifested. So religion binds one with the source i.e., God. One who understands religion is realising God. Religion is the highest expression of God and my religion is universal love and it includes all and excludes none." Would world religions accept it ? If accepted, the problem is solved, the way is cleared for a New Era. "Men must now unite in one religious fold, for in this way alone lies their salvation. The schisms and clashes, the strifes and wars, that continuously destroy human peace and happiness on this earth can only be eliminated when all persons of different religions express their desire to be incorporated in one universal Religion. This is the Plan of God" (Rishi Ram Ram).

Can there be anything more sublime, more noble more elevating than Love, for God is Love. Love is God's greatest instrument. It is the mightiest of Cosmic forces. It is the seed of Altruism. It is the fuel that feeds the flame of righteousness. It is the parent of all virtues. It is radiance par excellence. It is the crown of life. It is life perfected by the light of God" (M.K. Spencer) Why not we adopt this simple religion of Love as Universal Religion?

Sri Swami Omkar teaches not so much by spoken words but by example, the beauty and power of silence. "The man of silence whose heart is fixed on God and whose mind is attuned to God, is more dynamic than an active man. The vibrations surging from the silent man absorbed in God have a terrific speed. They cover a long vista of life and create a transformation of unusual order. It is misleading to think that inaction is a sin. When a man attains the highest spiritual state his inaction is of the most dynamic type. He becomes a vibratory force, whose currents reach the furthermost ends of the existing plane and help in creating an atmosphere of radiant health and beauty, peace and vitality of superb order. Sages and seers are the pillars in the vast emporium of life. They are the conductors of life giving energy to the atrophied and stale body of the human masses. (Rishi Ram Ram).

'Cosmic Flashes' contains good thoughts, simple stories and interesting illustrations from personal experience from the pen of a *Jeevan Muktha* i.e., Swamiji, which will be helpful in guiding as Practical Vedantha for all aspiring souls.

Swamiji's simple and unostentatious life is a saga of Humility, Sacrifice and Love. Says Swamiji, "My heart longs to share with you only what I personally experience in my daily life and not quotations from Vedas and Bible. My book of personal experience is my Veda. By His Grace I was blessed with a Heart of Universality that lives and feels for all, excluding none but includes all the Children of God in all the world." His life is a fulfillment of the threefold message of Gita viz. Serve — Love — Give. Yagna as a means to spiritual attainment is given in the Gita. Says Rishi Ram Ram. "Yagna is the sacrifice of the self at the Altar of the Divine. The lower self has to be utterly sacrificed before the higher self can grow. How do you sacrifice the lower self? By gradually giving away your pet prejudices and always by killing your desires. This is the great sacrifice ordained for spiritual progress. You understand that sacrifice is not killing or murder, but a constructive development towards the spiritual goal of Divine Evolution."

But swamiji has given a new dimension to that blessed word 'Sacrifice', when he offered his leg bone to another in need. Does he stop there? No. He further says, "Oh children of God? Here are my flesh, blood and bones. Here is my mind, heart and soul. Pray, do come to share my infinite love." It is in this way he teaches us to eradicate selfishness, the root cause of all misery in our world.

The presentation of Gita reveals the gradual ascending steps in the evolutionary process of the human soul in its march towards the ultimate goal — God realisation. In the same way, Swamiji takes us step by step to the goal if we can scan and scrutinize his Birth day messages from year to year. Space does not permit me to reproduce all of them here. "There are three things in Vedic language, very easy to repeat, but very difficult to feel them. They are Omnipresence, Omnipotence and Omniscience. Understand the real spirit behind these life-giving and soul-stirring Vedic aphorisms. You people generally repeat like parrots. The bubble comes from the wave, wave comes from the ocean. Wave is the world and Ocean is God. May we feel His Omnipresence, Omnipotence and Omniscience like the unbroken flow of oil poured from one vessel to another and let all be happy." Another soul-elevating truth Swamiji gives is:

"When God is within, why look outside?
When God is without, why look within?"

By this epistle Swamiji is initiating us into the sublime mystery of the *Vishwa-Rupa-Darshana* Yoga expounded by the World Teacher Lord Krishna, the Gita-Acharya. This shows us the way to liberation through life and activity here and now.

The above truth is expressed by Sri Swami Sivananda in a slightly different way so that common man can grasp easily, in a conversation that took place between Swamiji and an American philosopher.

"Have you seen God Swamiji? Asked American Philosopher Dr. Thomson."

"I see nothing but God", replied Swami Sivanandaji.

"In the food I take;
In the water I drink;
In the people I greet;
In the animals I meet;
And in you, Dr. Thomson;
I see nothing but God."

The doctrine of rebirth is a corrollary to the Law of Karma. *Karma* is a Sanskrit word that signifies action or deed. Any physical or mental action is *Karma*. Wherever there is a cause, an effect must be produced. The world runs on this fundamental law. This is inexorable and immutable. The doctrine of Reincarnation is as old as Vedas. Swamiji affirms this Law of *Karma* and reincarnation when he says, "Reincarnation is a simple Law and an open secret." In his small booklet entitled, '*The Re-incarnation of My Little Sister*', Swamiji tells us how his dear departed little sister has returned to him again in the form of Gnaneswari — now Mathaji Gnaneswari — Swamiji's Spiritual Heir.

Sri Swamiji's Life was a happy and harmonious blending of *Bhakti-Karma-Gnana*. The Temple of Lord Siva on a small hillock in enthralling surroundings enflames the latent devotion in every one of us. His inspiring Birthday Message "*Bolo Ram Karo Kam*", is a whip to every one of us to take to service, to our fellowmen — *Nishkam seva* i.e., service without craving for fruits. Our world is in need of such Karma Yogis. Sri Swami Vivekananda may be looked upon as a prince of yogis. He is not only a brilliant exponent of Karma yoga, but a very fine specimen of a *Bhakta*, a *Gnani* and *Karmayogi*. Swami Omkar prescribes: "If you want to be miserable think of yourself. If you want to be happy think of others", Sri Ram Ram teaches the same truth when he says, "(1) we are all servants of God Almighty and every moment of our life should be lived intensively in a spirit of unselfish Service. (2) Goodness means service to others, and you cannot live a good and happy life except through the happiness of others secured by all acts of service. So my message to you is, "Always think and live in a spirit of service".

PRAYER
(FOR WORLD PEACE)

ADORABLE PRESENCE!

Thou Who art within and without, above and below and all around, Thou Who art interpenetrating the very cells of our beings, Thou Who art the Eye of our eyes, Ear of our ears, Thou Who art the Heart of our hearts, Mind of our minds, Breath of our breaths, Life of our lives and Soul of our souls, bless us Dear God, to be aware of Thy Presence, NOW and HERE. This is all that we ask of THEE!

May all be aware of Thy Presence in the East and the West, in the North and the South! May PEACE and GOODWILL abide among individuals as well as communities and nations! This is our earnest prayer!

May Peace be unto all !

OM ! OM ! OM !

— *Swami Omkar*

Please help us by repeating this prayer often.

COMMENTARY

Dear Reader:

While SRI SWAMI OMKARJI was spending his time in the wilderness fasting and praying, this PRAYER was conceived in a moment of great inspiration, in the solitudes of Himalayas.

This prayer is a golden link, uniting the individual with the Universal and is precious and sacred to the Indwelling Presence of the heart, as it invokes blessings for all the people in East, West, North and South.

As you fervently repeat this Prayer, you begin to feel the Presence of God, in the Eye, Ear, Heart, Mind, Breath, Life and Soul. Verily. HE IS INTERPENETRATING THE VERY CELLS OF YOUR BEING.

As you come to the words : BLESS ME DEAR GOD—pause for a moment and perceive HIS OMNIPRESENCE both within and without. Pause at the words: PEACE and GOODWILL, and affirm Peace within and Goodwill among nations.

At the end, close your eyes, forget the outer world and merge within and thus taste the Peace that passeth all understanding in the stillness of your own purified heart.

— Sushila Devi

YOUR PEACE IS MY PEACE

May I have the privilege of serving you, to help yourself to establish PEACE in your heart and radiate It in your home, converting it into a HEAVEN or PEACE!

May you express PEACE in thought, word and deed, thus help to vibrate IT, from heart to heart, in the community, nation and the world at large, until PEACE pervades and permeates the whole universe, through your IDEAL LIFE OF PEACE!

This is the prayer of your brother Omkar.

—*Swami Omkar*

OM OM OM

PRAYER

"O God, we pray that we may be soon launched into a New Era of one World Religion, one World Polity, one World Civilisation, one World Humanity based on the foundations of equality and brotherhood, service and co-operation.

We pray that our scientists may now begin to study the inner worlds and give us the benefit of their researches. It is not only the union of all mankind that we seek, but the union of the whole universe, the discarnate co-operating with the incarnate spirits for the glory of Thy Kingdom. It is by means of universal love and prayers, that we shall build up a new kingdom of the spirit."

(Late) Yogi M.K. SPENCER
Author of 'HOW I FOUND GOD'

(Circulated by: DIVINE CENTRE, 7/250, Nehru Street, Markapur (A.P.)
SAI DIVINE RESEARCH CENTRE, 126, Sector 37, Faridabad.)

SIGNIFICANCE OF SWAMI OMKAR'S
PEACE PRAYER

(Inhale and Exhale Peace, as it is the Individual Peace that leads to Universal Peace)

THE Four Vedas are the four limbs of Hinduism, and the Upanishad are the essence of the Vedas. Of all the Upanishads the Kena Upanishad is considered to be one of the most important Upanishad, teaching the Transcendental Truth in a most lucid and simple manner. In it is found the following Mantram, or Holy Affirmation.

> "That Brahman is called *Tadvanam*. By the name of *Tadvanam*, IT is to be meditated upon. All love him who knows IT thus."

'*Tadvanam*' means: *Adorable of all*. By the name of Adorable it is to be meditated upon. How wonderful it is to see that our PEACE PRAYER begins with the Holy word *Tadvanam*: *Adorable Presence!* All Glory belongs to the Adorable Presence, Who is the life and the Soul of all existence and expression!

> "What is that thing by knowing which everything is known?"

has been the voice of the Sacred Vedas.

> "First seek Ye, The Kingdom of Heaven and his Righteousness and all these things shall be added unto you",

has been the call of the Holy Bible.

This Peace Prayer being Universal satisfies the *Dwaithi* — the Dualist, *Visistadwaiti* — the qualified Monist and the *Adwaiti* —the Monist. When you begin the Prayer with *Tadvanam* calling God as *Adorable Presence*, you are a Dualist. When you repeat the life giving words:

"Thou who art within, without, above, below and All around", you are a qualified Monist. When you come to repeat the soul-awakening words:

> *"Thou who art the Heart of the heart, Mind of the mind, Breath of the breath, Life of the life and the Soul of the soul, you are a Monist of the Highest order."*

You are establishing Peace in your individual heart when you are repeating:

> "Bless me Dear God! To be aware of thy Presence now and here is all that I ask of thee."

You are paving the way to Universal Peace, when you are repeating:

> "May all be aware of Thy Presence in the East and the West, the North and the South. May peace and Goodwill abide among individuals as well as communities and nations is my earnest prayer! May Peace be unto all! OM! OM! OM!"

The happy ending of the prayer with the three OMs, represents: *Omnipresence, Omnipotence* and *Omniscience*, covering the Past, Present and Future, thus establishing Peace and Goodwill, Now and forever on the rocky foundation of personal experience of Individual Peace, which is bound to be the greatest blessing to the Peace of the world.

In the same Kena Upanishad, we are happy to read the following soul-stirring words which are the essence of the Peace Prayer!

> He is the Ear of the ear, the Mind of the mind, the Speech of the speech. He is also the *Prana* of the *Prana*, the Eye of the eye. Knowing this, the wise, having relinquished all false identification of the Self with senses, become Immortal when departed from this world.

Thus the *Peace Prayer* satisfies every seeker of Truth all over the world. This Peace Prayer need not be confined to the East or the West, for it is a Prayer coming from within, from the heart of every man and woman, of every Religion and Nationality. Verily, the *Jiva*, the individual is striving to identify with the *Brahman*, one's own Heritage and thus express and assert his Divine Birthright of the Splendour of Millions of Suns.

This simple but most efficacious Prayer may be repeated by one and all, not only in English but in any language which is dear and near to one's heart. Its benefit and efficacy cannot be described in words, but can only be felt by each and every one, by mere repetition, not in the dim and distant future but immediately as it is being repeated. Hence, my Loving Readers of Peace, to make our theme complete let us feel in tune with the *Infinite* and repeat the *Peace Prayer* now.

OM! OM! OM!

SECTION II

1

INHALE AND EXHALE PEACE

Peace is our Birthright,
The Soul is Peace,
SANTHOYAM ATMA—
External Bliss.

Born in the sanctum of heart
Your life can be full of peace,
Full of glory and poise,
On your forehead God's kiss.

God's kiss on your front,
No trouble now and here,
Your world — a lake of peace
Waveless and clear.

Peace is the birthright of every Soul, nay, the Soul is Peace. *Santhoyam Atma*, says the Upanishad. He who practises this Mantram would realise God not in the remote future, but here and now. With every inhalation of yours try to take in Peace, and try to give out Peace only, with every exhalation. Your very life should become Peace. He who feels this Peace that is all-pervasive, experiences it not only in the inner-most sanctum of his heart and to the very marrow of his bones, but *everywhere* outside too. For him the whole world becomes one vast undisturbed Lake of Peace. The troubles and conflicts, the misery and exploitation, the sin and shortcomings that are apparent everywhere cease to exist for him. Eternal poise and everlasting stability are his. He who thus realizes Peace realizes God, for verily the two are one.

☆☆☆ OM TAT SAT OM ☆☆☆

2

RELIGION AND LIFE ARE ONE

God is one. He is without a second.
Worship of God is high religious life,
For He is all-in-all, eternal truth.
Blessed is he, who lives in Him — there is no strife.

God is one. He is without a second—*Ekameva advitiyam*. He is the All. Religion is the worship of God, the worship of All. As such, religion and life are not two but one. For the sage, religion is life and life is religion. To live integrally is to live religiously. God is Love, and hence to live religiously is to live as Love. Blessed is the soul that has realized this Truth.

☆☆☆ OM TAT SAT OM ☆☆☆

3

EXISTENCE, KNOWLEDGE AND BLISS ABSOLUTE

Merge in the ocean, in the Absolute.
Forget yourself.
For you are nothing — and yet all,
Brahman Itself.

The Absolute, *Brahman*, is the ocean. Vast, deep and fathomless it is. Creation is the wave. The individuals are the bubbles. In the ocean there is nothing but existence, wisdom and bliss. When the bubble bursts it merges with this ocean of *Sat-chit-ananda*. Unlimited bliss and infinite awareness are its possession, nay it becomes THAT.

And what then is the possession and who is the possessor? This is to be experienced in silence. Inadequate are words to express it. But this experience does not become complete till it is achieved both in contemplation and work.

For the *Brahman* is the invisible as well as the visible, the unmanifested as well as the manifested yet it transcends both.

☆☆☆ OM TAT SAT OM ☆☆☆

4

DELUSION OF THE SNAKE AND ROPE

God is the real, existing alone,
The rest is Maya.
Why run after delusion? Let it be gone!
Your birthright is Ananda.

The Real and the unreal never both existed. They do not and will not coexist. There was only one at the beginning, the true. And the true it is that exists and will exist. *"Sat eva Somya idam agra isith"* The not-true never existed, does not exist and cannot exist in the future also. God alone exists, nothing else exists outside or apart from Him.

Art thou God or nothing? Thou art God, for nothing exists not. Enough of the illusion and the running after the mirage. Recognize either the rope or the snake. Together both of them cannot abide. Enough unto the day of the snake-idea. Thou hast suffered enough on account of it. Realize now the rope, the one Reality, God.

☆☆☆ OM TAT SAT OM ☆☆☆

5

ALL IS GOD

All is God, the Cosmic Source
In East and West.
Why always struggle? Surrender yourself.
In God is rest.

God is the All. Wherever you turn your eyes to the east, south, west or north, it is God whom you behold. Above, below, on every side it is the Divine that envelopes you. *Brahma eva idam amrtam purastath, Brahma paschat, Brahma dakshinatacha uttarascha.* It is from the Divine that wisdom as well as ignorance originate. Then why this struggle? Why these prayers and meditations, these fasts and mutterings of the Mantra? The struggle too is an illusion. For who forsooth is the struggler, and with whom and for what is he struggling? Give up therefore all struggles. Surrender yourself to the Infinite and abide in Silence.

☆☆☆ OM TAT SAT OM ☆☆☆

6

SUNDAY, THE DAY OF SUNSHINE

Sunday — the day of the sun!
Let the sun of the Soul too shine bright.
Let the clouds be always dispelled.
Be established forever in light!

Today is a Sunday, the day of the Sun of Light resplendent. I am always happy on a Sunday, for it is the day of rest and relaxation. It is the day on which worldly affairs are put aside.

But why have a Sunday once a week only? Why not let every day be a Sunday, a day of light, prayer and peace, a day of relaxation? Let the Sun of the Soul shine forth, let the clouds that veil the Sun be dispelled. *"Tatvam pushan apavrunu satyadharmaya dhrishtaye"*. May we be established and centred in the Sun for ever.

☆☆☆ OM TAT SAT OM ☆☆☆

7

FREEDOM FROM FOREIGN MATTER

Let your mind stand still and be calm,
All desire is vanished and gone.
Saturated with truth,
Freedom you have won.

It is days since I have taken food or water. I feel weak but at the same time I feel free and light. Really, contemplation is possible only when the mind runs not after this and that affair, and the body craves not for food and raiment. When the mind stands still, undisturbed and calm, it is saturated with truth. *Yoga chittavritti nirodhah.* No prayer or meditation is necessary. No effort is needed. Sit thou still, calm and pure. It is to the pure and the childlike that Heaven belongs.

☆☆☆ OM TAT SAT OM ☆☆☆

8

CHARGE YOUR BATTERY WITH GOD-HOOD

Open your eyes and see
Light and eternal love!
Open your eyes and feel
Eternal Bliss from above!

Man is like a battery. If he is aware of God, the battery is. charged; if not, like the discharged battery he is lifeless. But the metaphor is not capable of complete application. While the battery requires the power to charge it from outside, the power that is to animate man is within himself. All that he has to do is to become aware of his eternal possession. He should only open his eyes and see that he is ever full of light, life and love.

☆☆☆ OM TAT SAT OM ☆☆☆

9

COSMIC CONSCIOUSNESS

Happiness lies in yourself.
So stay in this god-like state,
Where finite becomes infinite!
Fling open the cosmic gate!

Beatitude or salvation is the cessation of all struggle, strife and conflict. In that state, the finite becomes the Infinite. But this state is not something to be acquired anew now. It is something which is possessed by every soul eternally. Only the Soul has forgotten its pristine glory and lives in an illusion. Like the man who has forgotten that the watch is on his wrist and searches for it in every other place and is sad because he finds it not, the Soul searches for happiness everywhere, forgetting that all happiness lies in Itself.

☆☆☆ OM TAT SAT OM ☆☆☆

10

LET THE SUN OF SUNS DISPEL THE CLOUDS

As the sun will rise after dawn,
Let the sun of your soul arise.
Dispelling all the dark clouds,
Let the sun of the suns make you wise.

It is dawn now. Darkness has not as yet vanished completely. The Sun has not yet risen. But he shall arise. There are signs of his advent. The "ushas" heralds him.

Let the Sun of your Soul also arise. Let Him dispel all the dark clouds of ignorance and egoism. May He shine in His glory parching up the little ponds of envy, malice, cruelty etc., and may He make the crops of happiness, goodwill and sweetness thrive!

☆☆☆ OM TAT SAT OM ☆☆☆

11

COME OUT OF THE CAGE OF BODY

You are not the body itself;
A cage it is for your Soul.
Cling not to the earthly bonds;
The boundless Breath is your goal.

Do you wish to be imprisoned forever in this small and lightless dungeon of flesh and blood that is the body — the physical body? Yearn you not for freedom? Wish you not to soar in the skies of delight, unfettered and free? Then, come out and feel yourself, in tune with the Infinite. How could the finite and the earthly give you unlimited happiness? Emerge from the small ego in which you are enmeshed and acquire Cosmic-consciousness.

Why do you identify yourself with this body, its joys and sorrows? Body-consciousness is the root of all misery. It is bondage. Cling not to this corpse, realise that you are the boundless, the *Brihat* and the vast, *Bhauman*.

☆☆☆ OM TAT SAT OM ☆☆☆

12

THE WHOLE WORLD IS IMAGINATION

The Invisible and Eternal is real,
This hold in your thoughts alone.
Don't think of your pain and suffering,
Live in God, and peace you have won.

Bondage and salvation are imaginations of the mind. Where is bondage in the Heights? Where is freedom there? Who has fettered you that you should think of freeing yourself? Where is the evil, the misery and the suffering that can trouble you, while all is joy? Worldly cares, ills of the body — say you? Where are they? Are not they chimeras you have yourself raised? Bondage and freedom, evil, and good, body and world — imagination these are all. It is the nature of thought to revel amidst these dualities and opposites. Unreal they are all. That which is beyond thought, that which is the Source of all things is the Real. It is You. It is the Inner Self, Changeless, Invisible and Eternal. May you realise your Essence and be established in THAT!

☆☆☆ OM TAT SAT OM ☆☆☆

13

THE RICHEST TREASURE — MYSELF

The Inner Self is my richest treasure.
I cannot lose it; it is my soul.
The Inner self is the Highest treasure,
To find it, to keep it — my only goal.

I am fortunate, for I have found the richest treasure. My treasure consists not in lands or buildings, in pounds or in any articles. My treasure lies in myself. I have found my Soul, in that I have acquired everything. The Self is the richest treasure in heaven or earth. Everything is desired for the sake of the Self — *Atmanah kamaya*. Self comes first and last and final. Having found it, verily have I found everything.

☆☆☆ OM TAT SAT OM ☆☆☆

14

YOU ARE ETERNALLY IN GOD

Can you forget God?
You live and breathe in Him.
Eternally you are in God.
He is your light within.

Have you forgotten God? Nay, it is impossible. How can you forget Him? You live and breathe in Him. You work and think in Him. For indeed there is not anything that in heaven, earth or hell that is not God! Forgetfulness of God! It is a contradiction. Whatever you think, do or say is of God and in God. So make not an effort to remember Him. Give up all effort and struggle. Do as you please or think whatever you please. Or sit still and do not think of anything. It is all one and the same, for you are eternally in God, as One without a second.

☆☆☆ OM TAT SAT OM ☆☆☆

15

VITALITY OF THREE KINDS

Be active as much as you can.
In Vitality centered in Peace,
Serene and immersed in it,
You'll win divinest bliss.

From every side you are asked to be not idle, to be doing something, to be active. You have to be active, vital. Yes, but what sort of activity, what kind of vitality? Is it the ever bustling activity of the modern industrial age or is it the slow but startling vitality of the panther or the cave-man? Neither; for the one is *rajasic* and the other *tamasic*. It is activity founded on calm, vitality centred in Peace that you should cultivate. "*Karmani akarmayah pasyeth, akarmanicha karmayah.*" Serene and immersed in inner Peace you should ever be. Active you should be also, but not for the sake of the ego. For the Divine and in the Divine should you be active. From there should your vitality be derived.

☆☆☆ OM TAT SAT OM ☆☆☆

16

SELF IS WITNESS OF ALL

Your thoughts are not your own,
Neither work, nor sleep, nor dream.
Self is witness of all.
Abandon yourself to Him.

When you do a thing think you that you do it? When you think a thought believe you that you are its author? When asleep you are, is it you that sleep? No. It is He, that is the Author of all action, that is the Master of all works *(Karmadyaksha).* Without Him the breeze stirs not, the fire crackles not, nor does the sun shine. *"Thasya bhasaa sarvamidam vibhathi."* When you are thinking it is He that thinks, when you are doing it is He that does. Meditate on Him and merge in Him. Yet, He is beyond speech and thought. What should one do then? Nothing. Abandon yourself utterly to Him, *"ekam saranam vraja."*

☆☆☆ OM TAT SAT OM ☆☆☆

17

THOUGHTS ARE THE RAYS OF THE SUN OF SUNS

The waves remain with the Ocean,
The rays are not separate from the sun,
And thoughts are the rays of Divinity.
Pasya me yogam aisvaram.

The Sun sheds his rays of light, everywhere — on all sides. But where do they go when he disappears. Do not they go with him? The ocean ceaselessly sends forth waves. Yet, is one single wave separated from the ocean and lost? No. The waves remain with the ocean, yet they are sent out. So too thoughts and deeds emanate from the Soul. But not one thought or deed is separate and aloof from the Soul. Their locus standi is the Soul. They are always in it. But yet they are not the Soul, just as the rays are not the sun and the waves are not the ocean. The Soul is unmanifested and manifested. Yet it is in neither. It transcends both. *"Pasya me yogam aisvaram"*.

☆☆☆ OM TAT SAT OM ☆☆☆

18

NO FORGETFULNESS IN GOD

Can I forget my God, my Soul?
Can I forget Him, my life?
Being in the chamber of my own Heart,
He is my help in each strife.

Can I forget God, who is the Life of my life and the Soul of my soul? But I am forgetting Him. Yet, am I not remembering Him even in my forgetfulness? Does not He sit like the unbidden guest in the chamber of my soul, whether I attend to Him or not? He is with me and in me always, whether I consciously remember the fact or not. Let me therefore cast aside the very idea that I could forget Him.

☆☆☆ OM TAT SAT OM ☆☆☆

19

INDIVIDUAL SAMADHI IS SELFISH

If you retire to meditate,
Don't drink the cup of samadhi alone.
Let you salvation be blessing for all.
Give from it, what you have won.

Do you wish to become a recluse in order to become a contemplative, enjoying bliss? Is it for you only that the joys of *Samadhi* are reserved? Yearn you not to take with you the millions of your sisters and brothers who are in the dark? Would you feed on the Divine when others are starving and parching for the lifegiving nourishment? Let your salvation be for the welfare of all, let your *Samadhi* be for the good of everybody.

☆ ☆ ☆ OM TAT SAT OM ☆ ☆ ☆

20

BREATH IS THE STRING OF LIFE

We all are beads, tied up to a string.
Countless we are, but the garland is one.
The string of life — it is our breath.
So one we are and never alone.

The individual is a bead. Countless are the beads. But the string that ties them up into a garland is one. On the Infinite is strung this garland of finite beings. "*Sutre mani gana iva.*" Engross not yourself with the beads, remember also the string which sustains them all. Fix your attention on it.

☆☆☆ OM TAT SAT OM ☆☆☆

21

NOTHING CAN BE ADDED TO OR TAKEN FROM COMPLETENESS

There is nothing for which I should anyhow crave
If I feel complete in a perfect way.
Nothing can be added or taken from it.
Completeness is perfect eternally.

There are moments when I feel complete in a perfect way. The present moment is one such. I do not wish to close my eyes and meditate, for what have I to gain thereby? Neither do I wish to open my eyes and gaze at the outer beauty. For how do I profit from it? Everything is complete and perfect. There is nothing for which I should crave, there is nothing that I should work, for I have been, always complete.

Suppose I do not recognise this perfection, this completeness and remain silent. Do I lose anything? Nothing whatsoever. Does the rock lose its rockiness, if it toils not? Does the rose forego its sweet beauty if it works not? Nothing can be added or subtracted from perfection by our exertions. *Purnamadhah Purnamidham, Purnaath Purnamudhachyate; Purnasya Purmadhaya Purnam eva avasishyate.* Realise that you are perfect and complete eternally. After that you may do or stop doing anything.

☆☆☆ OM TAT SAT OM ☆☆☆

22

HOW BREATH DESTROYS THE EGO

The ego is the root of lust of passion and greed,
Destroy it with stalk, with branch and with root.
Inhaling, exhaling the breath divine,
And divine you are, a spark of God.

The ego is at the root of all troubles. From it comes lust, passion, greed and anger. So long as the ego remains, the individual *(jiva)* has no peace. Only when the ego is annihilated — root, stalk and branch, can there be peace.

How to destroy this ego? Identify yourself with the Infinite, the Divine. Realise that you are That. "*Soham*". With every breath you take in and every breath you exhale, concentrate on this truth of "*Soham*" or "That I am". The "*Soham*" will annihilate all that is restless, fickle and changing.

☆☆☆ OM TAT SAT OM ☆☆☆

23

CERTAIN THINGS YOU HAVE TO DO YOURSELF

Hear on your innermost being,
Don't hear on the things of outside,
Let your own soul be glorious,
Overflow of your own light.

My writing table is clustered with all kinds of junk. All sorts of books and dictionaries, pens and papers crowd it. But can I rely on these books to write something? If I rely on them it will be the writing of the authors of those books and not mine. How will it be my writing, my message? If you have something to express, express it straight from your innermost being. Whatever you do, think or say, let it be a spontaneous outglowing of your Soul. Rely not on the things of outside. Whatever Plato thought and said, whatever Kant thought and said, whatever Vyasa or Valmiki wrote is contained within you also. Dam it not, allow your Soul to flow and wash away all dirt and sins.

☆☆☆ OM TAT SAT OM ☆☆☆

24

THE ONE UNIVERSAL ENERGY

There is one Energy working in all,
Working in the sun, in the sea.
Be aware of its Presence, its changeless form.
It is working in you and in me.

The sources of energy may seem many, the Sun, the water-falls, the sea, electricity etc. But ultimately there is only one Energy in all of them. It is the same Energy that is in the Niagara and in the sea. It is the very same Energy that is in me and is now making me think and write. Nothing is done without its support and sanction.

When you are thinking and scheming it is THAT which is thinking and scheming in you. So there is nothing to worry about or feel sorry for. Only be aware of the Presence in silence and activity, in ebb and flow, in joy and pain, in health and sickness. When you cognise the Changeless in change, you will be blessed with Peace and Cosmic Joy.

☆☆☆ OM TAT SAT OM ☆☆☆

25

THE SOUL IS ABOVE THOUGHT

Being thinking, being praying,
It is God, working through you.
As the waves are the ocean, arising or calm,
So your soul is God, living in you.

Are you sorry that you do not find time to pray and meditate? Are you worried that you have to think out so much and do so many things? What is it that does or think, when you do or think of something? Is it not God that is working through you? In what way do you become less by thinking and doing and more by not thinking and not doing? Whether the waves rise a hundred feet high or do not rise at all, it is still the ocean. Similarly whether you are praying in church or working in office, it is God who works in and through you always.

☆☆☆ OM TAT SAT OM ☆☆☆

26

A THOUSAND-MILE JOURNEY STARTS WITH THE FIRST STEP

Everything starts with the first step ahead,
Whatever we need, we'll have it in time.
The treasures of God, be on all sides,
Rely on Him, trust in Him, trust the Divine.

Even a thousand-mile journey starts with the first step. Today I have accidentally come in possession of a single Dollar Bill. I feel so rich. Even a million dollars begin with one Dollar. And that I have now. If I use what I have, what I have will grow. Everything else I need will be added unto it in its own good time. Talents are not to be buried but to be used.

Divine plenty surrounds all of us. Untold treasures of God lie on all sides of us. We have only to trust and believe in the Divine Providence. Whatever we need will be vouchsafed to us at the proper time. May we learn to rely on the Divine.

☆☆☆ OM TAT SAT OM ☆☆☆

27

AT LAST SAHAJA SAMADHI
God Consciousness

*Let me merge in **Samadhi**, in this blessed state,*
In God-consciousness, where all struggles fade,
In God-vision, that neither comes nor goes,
Eternally present, where bliss and peace rule.

At last *'sahaja samadhi'* or the state of God-vision. It may not be permanent. Why not? But can it be only temporary or transitory? Is it not a blessed state which neither comes nor goes, but is eternally present?

In *samadhi*, all strife and struggle ceases. One is free from all prayer and meditation, mind-control and fasts. All duties disappear. Things done are done and finished. Things to be done do not appear. One feels free, light and irresponsible like a dry leaf. One becomes aloof and detached from all things like the dry coconut in which the shell has become separate from the kernel.

☆☆☆ OM TAT SAT OM ☆☆☆

28

THE ATMAN IS THE OCEAN

Myself is the Atman, myself is the ocean,
Myself is a drop, a wave all in motion.
I never am separate, being part of the whole,
The Cosmos is throbbing in my heart, in my soul.

Myself or Atman is the ocean. In this ocean of reality that is perfection, this world is a mere wave, and the organism a mere drop in the wave. The ordinary man when he is thinking or acting thinks that this body, this drop is acting. But for the God-man, the drop is only a component in the wave and the wave only a part of the ocean. Every drop, however tiny it may be, is it separate from the ocean that is the whole?

In every beat of his heart, the wise man recognises the cosmic throbbing, in every action and thought of his, he sees the Universal Action.

☆☆☆ OM TAT SAT OM ☆☆☆

29

THE INDIVISIBLE BREATH

In whatever we do, it is the Spirit in all,
In the Universe, in me and in you the same call,
The Source of all breath, all sound, speech and sight
Is the Infinite, Tat-twam-asi — eternal Light.

Is it the eye that sees, when I see? Is it the ear that hears when I hear? And is it the tongue that tastes when I eat? It is the Spirit, the very same Spirit that is in me, is in you and the universe, that sees, hears and tastes. Be conscious of this Universal Witness the Indivisible Breath in every action of yours and in your inaction too. Forget the little "I" and the "My". Remember constantly the Source of all breath, speech, sight, touch and sound. In whatever we do, it is the Infinite that is expressing itself. It is That which is fulfilling itself in and through this world of things.

☆☆☆ OM TAT SAT OM ☆☆☆

30

OUT OF THE DEPTHS FRESH STRENGTH

Of the depths fresh strength, of the dark new light
As tests are in life so are clouds at the sky.
Through struggles and sorrows we are on the way;
Don't mind thorns, fix your gaze on the aim.

Inspiring is the thought contained in these wise words of Abraham Lincoln.

So long as we are in the body, there is some trouble or other. That is inevitable. Show me the sky without its clouds and the rose without its thorns. Similarly, there is no life without its tests and tribulations. Life is a process of silent, slow and steady growth towards the Goal, through struggles and sorrows. Mind not the thorns and the pebbles, the pitfalls and the snares on the way. Have your gaze fixed, your attention rivetted on the Goal. Remember that no amount of obstacles can prevent you from reaching the Goal. If you are determined about it, it is destined for you.

☆☆☆ OM TAT SAT OM ☆☆☆

31

EGOISM

Root out the ego, its is like the seeds,
Dormant in the earth, sprouting out when rain greets,
Root out it utterly, looking at your own faults;
To see faults in others — you are not called.

To root out the ego is a difficult task. Often it looks as though it is absent. But when the test comes, out it emerges, like those seeds which lie dormant throughout summer under the earth, but sprout out as soon as the rains come.

The ego covers up our own faults, goes afinding faults in others. It forgets the beams in its own eyes, but sees motes in others' eyes. If you want real Peace, utterly abandon the ego.

☆☆☆ OM TAT SAT OM ☆☆☆

32

ALL THE WORLD IS BRAHMAN

All the world is God, be aware of Him,
Who is in all, in the holy and the sin,
In the fallen and the risen, in the living and the dead
Be aware of Him — that is the highest state.

All this is *Brahman*. All the world is God. Every thing we see is part of His manifestation. The Peace that passeth all understanding belongs only to those rare souls, for whom every one and everything appears as a manifestation of the One God.

It is rather difficult to be aware of God in the ugly, in the sinful, in the ghastly and the cruel. Yet, God is as much in it as in the beautiful, the noble and the holy. To be aware of the one God in the fallen and the risen, the dead and the living, in the crucifixion as well as in the resurrection, is the highest state.

☆☆☆ OM TAT SAT OM ☆☆☆

33

YOU ARE THE INTELLIGENCE

You are not the body, be happy and free.
Be a witness in life, all comes through Prakriti.
Don't care for the world, whether darkness or light
Whether health or illness. Eternal witness your guide.

It has been my habit for years to wake up at dawn and begin the day with the reading of the *Ashtavakra Gita*. It was yesterday morning that I read this verse, "*You are not the body, neither is the body yours. You are Consciousness, the Eternal witness. Hence be free and happy.*"

What a wonderful thought that is! But how difficult it is to follow it! Whether it be sorrow or happiness, whether it be prosperity or adversity, whether it be health or illness, the *Ashtavakra* asks us to stand aloof and look upon them as only a witness. What happens is due to *Prakriti*. What have I, the Eternal seer, the Witness, to do with it?

Today I did not read the *Ashtavakra Gita*. Why should I read it any more? In the above verse is contained the whole truth. Enough if we practise this truth.

☆☆☆ OM TAT SAT OM ☆☆☆

34

AMIDST THE CLOUDS OR STUMBLING BLOCKS

As shadows of sorrow are the clouds on the sun
Don't trouble yourself, if you are standing alone.
The darkest clouds, they will pass, will melt away.
They'll disappear before Sun's mighty ray.

Are you unhappy? Have your trust and love been misplaced, have your kindness and hospitality been misused, have false accusations and calumny been raised against you? Sorrow not. When all is well, everyone can be cheerful and contented. He alone is brave who stands towering amidst misery and gloom.

You are the Self, the effulgent Sun. You are not this corpse, this body. Troubles and sorrows may cast their shadows upon you, as do clouds upon the Sun. But the darkest clouds will pass, they will melt away and disappear before the resplendent glory of the Sun.

☆☆☆ OM TAT SAT OM ☆☆☆

35

BE SWEET

Never cease shedding love, though you are hurt,
Live in the Atman in deed and in word.
Be like the rose, smelling so sweet,
Though trampled and crushed — sow out love's seed.

Repent not of having done good. You may be hurt, kicked and crushed under iron heels mercilessly. Still continue doing good. Blessed are they that are persecuted and fallen, for they shall be raised and exalted.

Let the arrogant, the haughty, the ignorant and the wicked hurt, wound and crush ruthlessly. But cease not shedding love, life and light towards them. Be like the rose that gives out sweet fragrance, though trampled. Remember that. Let no one repent of doing good!

☆☆☆ OM TAT SAT OM ☆☆☆

36

THE PRESENT MOMENT

Waste not the moment, the present is your power,
Waste it not, use it, utilise each hour.
Don't look to the future, don't think of the past,
In tune with the Infinite be peaceful atlast.

Waste not the present moment. In it consists your supreme wealth. The present is your highest moment. As such waste it not, treasure it up, hug it. But how can you utilise it to the utmost? You can make the fullest use of it by attuning yourself with the Infinite, by abandoning yourself to the Divine, this moment.

☆☆☆ OM TAT SAT OM ☆☆☆

37

LOVE IS THE UNFAILING REMEDY

God's shining everywhere in unceassing love,
God's shining from each face with light from above.
Surrender to him, see His sweet loving face,
Surrender to him in love's shining rays.

I have the vision, yea, I have it. After passing through the terrible Gethsemane of excruciating mental struggle, agony and suffering I am glad to say that I have won and that I have the Vision.

I give up now all struggle and strain. I have nothing now to achieve, nothing to long for. I surrender myself to Love, Universal Love. No more is any one an enemy or evil-doer to me. All are the living images of God. All is love, abundance and forgiveness now. No more are resentment and self-defence; no more any of those self-righteous arguments. Everywhere I see the face of the Deity, for all is God.

God is shining from every face!

☆☆☆ OM TAT SAT OM ☆☆☆

38

IMPOSSIBLE TO FORGET GOD

I'm living in God, for He is my life.
In trials, in tests, in sickness, in strife,
In sleep and in dream, never absent from Him,
In Samadhi saturated—His glory I sing!

How can I be away from God when whatever I think or do is of Him! If I am quiet it is He. If I am bustling and hustling it is He. If I am healthy it is He. Even in sickness it is He. In all tests, trials and tribulations it is He. Where then is the moment when He is away, aloof or absent from me? In sleep, in wakefulness and in dream it is He. And it is He again in *Samadhi*.

How glorious! Every sound expresses Him. Every sight portrays Him. Every manifestation springs from Him. I am privileged to be saturated and surrounded by His glory.

☆☆☆ OM TAT SAT OM ☆☆☆

39

THE LOWER AND THE HIGHEST SELF

Two natures in you are living, lower and higher self.
They are fighting and struggling, ineffable, their strength.
Will you go to perdition? Or take the right way?
The last leads to Heaven, see you the holy ray?

Man is bipolar. In him there are two natures—the lower and the higher, the animal and the divine. The two are incessantly fighting to win over man. The lower nature tries to drag man to the life of the senses, to perdition. The higher nature longs to lead man towards the life of Reason, to Heaven. Wisdom consists in giving one's assent to the higher nature and co-operating with it.

☆☆☆ OM TAT SAT OM ☆☆☆

40

THE PRESENCE IS ABOVE FORGETFULNESS

Why do we not feel God's Presence always,
Though longing for it each moment, all days?
Remember, His Presence is always there.
Don't worry, for ever you are in His care.

Sometimes one feels the presence of God, sometimes not. What is wrong? Why does not one feel the Presence always in each and every moment?

This feeling or not feeling is all the imagination of the restless mind. The awareness of the Presence is beyond remembrance and forgetfulness. The Presence is always there. It is the one supreme fact. There is no second thing. So you cannot forget IT and remember something else. No one need therefore worry about not remembering God's Presence.

☆☆☆ OM TAT SAT OM ☆☆☆

41

LET THE CENTRE BE WITHIN

Be established in self, be centered in Him,
Hold fast to the Self in thick and in thin.
Don't depend on the world, don't depend on a friend.
The Centre within is your holy land.

You may have mastered the principles of all religions and philosophies, still you cannot avoid having moments of depression, heaviness and sorrow. That is so because your perceptions and conceptions are not centred in the Self. Unconsciously at least the centre is for the time being placed outside. It is shifted from within to without, hence is all this helplessness, agony and suffering.

If you want to be perpetually happy, there is but one way to follow. Be established in the Self, be centred in the Self. Through thick and thin hold fast to the Self. The outside thing that attracts you may be a big and mighty person or thing, but depend not on it. Unruffled peace belongs only to those who are centred in SELF.

☆☆☆ OM TAT SAT OM ☆☆☆

42

THE CAUSE IS WITHIN

Be a sun, radiating everywhere your clear light;
Spread your happiness, cheerfulness far and wide.
Make the best and the highest with godlike thought;
In yourself is the cause, your luck and your fault.

If you are happy and cheerful, you will radiate happiness and cheerfulness around you, as the Sun does the light. If you are sorrowful and miserable, like the noxious weed which scatters its foul smell all around, you will spread your sorrow and misery.

But it is a comfort and consolation to know that your joy and sorrow are not wrought by outside factors. You are the sole and sufficient cause of your happiness and unhappiness, your health and sickness. You need not invoke any outside power or deity. All that you have to do is to realise that you, the Self, are beyond dualities and thought, and all things are nothing but an expression of your will *(ichcha)*. As such, you can change all your negative thought into positive and assert only the Best and the Highest under all conditions.

☆☆☆ OM TAT SAT OM ☆☆☆

43

BE NATURAL

Don't torture yourself, don't carry a cross.
God is within you, He is all your force.
You'll find Him in silence, you'll find Him in sound.
With Him you're eternally united and sound.

I have been guilty now and then of torturing myself with difficult austerities. I have mercilessly injured my body at times, innumerable crosses have I carried. But is all this necessary? When God is within as well as without, pervading and permeating through all my countless cells, why should I torture myself with restless practices? If the state of *samadhi* or trance occurs to me naturally it is alright. But why on earth should I force it on myself? Is not God as much in wakefulness as in trance? If I cannot find Him in Silence, in Sound I shall find Him.

If I fail to express His glory in meditation, in work I shall express Him. It is in Him and by Him that I walk, talk and write. From Him, the Unmanifested, is all expression and manifestation. Be it work or meditation, one thing is certain. I am inseparably and eternally united with Him.

☆☆☆ OM TAT SAT OM ☆☆☆

44

NO MORE FORGETFULNESS

Oh God, have I lost you? I'm helpless and sad!
For if I forget you, I cannot be glad.
No, no, you are penetrating my heart and my soul,
Your light is within me, above and below.

The least forgetfulness of God or the Light within, even if it is for a millionth of a second, makes me miserable, helpless and sad. But what is forgetfulness? Do not memory and forgetfulness come from Him? The Light of lights is eternally present, penetrating to the very core of my being and pervading through the whole universe.

It is not possible to forget God and remember something else. For what is that which is not He? That He could be forgotten is only an illusive thought.

Behold, the all-present Light is here, there, within without, above, below and on all sides. Whichever way you turn, you are under its illuminating rays. Never can you be in the dark. Recognize this and be silent once for all. Delude not yourself with the illusive thought of forgetfulness.

☆☆☆ OM TAT SAT OM ☆☆☆

45

IN THE WORLD OF GOD-CONSCIOUSNESS

Be always in me, let me live in Your Light,
In Your all-pervasive Presence, in Your world so bright.
And now You are here and filling my heart,
God-consciousness is my eternal part.

I cannot wait for God to come to me later on. Unbearable to me is the thought that God is not now with me and that He will come to me in the uncertain future. I need not even meditate to attain God. If God is not already in and around me, whence does He come?

He is here and everywhere. He is enternally one with me. All that I have to do is only to be aware of His all-pervasive Presence. Even if I am not in His Presence consciously, yet I am and have been always in Him.

☆☆☆ OM TAT SAT OM ☆☆☆

46

GOD-REALIZATION NOW AND HERE

God-realization now and here.
You never need search Him, His voice you can hear.
Now open your eyes and feel Ananda.
He is eternally realized, ***nitya siddha.***

God-realization now and here. Now and here? Is not full and complete eternally? Have spatial and temporal modes of speaking any reference to this supreme and eternal fact? Was there a time when God was non-existent and will there be ever such? I have been, am and will always abide in perfection, in God's Presence. He is eternally realized, *nitya siddha*.

There is no need to shut your eyes to search for Him within. Open your eyes, for He is here. You need not wait for Him, for He has been eternally in quest of you.

☆☆☆ OM TAT SAT OM ☆☆☆

47

RELIGION IS REALIZATION OF CHEERFULNESS

Religion is realization, cheerful hilarity.
Let your soul be smiling, singing His beauty.
Come face to face with God, expressing the Divine,
He is ***Anando Brahma****, infinite-sublime!*

Aflame is my Soul, bubbling I am with laughter. Yes, why not? Religion is realization. Realization is laughter. Religion does not mean to remain with a long, sad and mournful face, muttering to yourself something within.

Religion means to come face to face with God, that is within and without. To express the Divine in this world of tests and trials is religion.

Anando Brahma. Bliss is God. He is there where the little self, the ego, has been rooted out. Egoism creates pride, passion and arrogance. Identification of the finite with Infinite kills pride, passion and arrogance and creates rippling Laughter in the Heart and Peace of the Soul.

☆☆☆ OM TAT SAT OM ☆☆☆

48

THE RESTLESS CHILD

In a trance of ecstasy I enjoyed highest Bliss,
Feeling in silence, in meditation, God's kiss.
But like restless child, descending from the height,
I want to share with you the rapturous light.

A little child, playful and restless, am I. The child sows a seed and no sooner has he covered it with earth, than he digs it up to see whether it has germinated. I close my eyes to contemplate and enjoy the Bliss Absolute in a trance of divine ecstasy. But no sooner do I begin feeding on the Divine, than I descend from the heights and begin to write, toying with inadequate words.

I long to bring within your reach all the fruit that I have begun to taste. I myself never wait until I finish eating the fruit in full. But what am I to do? Helpless I am in subduing my burning desire to share with you all my experiences. It is sweet no doubt to sit all day long in silent contemplation and rapturous ecstasy. But I evade it. May I be of some use to many a weary and aspiring soul.

☆☆☆ OM TAT SAT OM ☆☆☆

The Pranava (OM) is the bow, the Atman is the arrow and the Brahman is said to be its mark. It should be hit by one who is self-collected and that which hits becomes like the arrow, one with the mark i.e. BRAHMAN.

☆☆☆ OM TAT SAT OM ☆☆☆

49

BEHOLD THE ONE IN THOUGHT

My God is everywhere, within and without;
He is in my heart, He is in my thought.
I see Him in others and in the whole world.
He is beyond my senses, speaking in each word.

I close my eyes to see Him. Again I open them to find Him; for is not He within and without too? Within He is in the depths of the heart, the marrows of the bone and cores of the cells. Without He is in every form and name.

But who is it that sees through these eyes? Who else can it be other than He, for there exists only He without a second. He it is that sees. He it is that is seen. He who sees the one in the many is blessed. But he who sees without seeing is privileged; for He is beyond sight, sound, smell, touch and taste.

☆☆☆ OM TAT SAT OM ☆☆☆

50

VOID CAN MAKE AND UNMAKE

In the beginning there was Void, creating Life and Mind.
Mind created good and evil in mankind.
Now never be restless, seek the one great Source;
Merge into Prana, into Void — the highest force.

In the beginning there was Void. From it emerged Life and from it arose Mind.

Mind is like a mischievous and intoxicated monkey. It is ever restless. But it has great power. It can make and unmake. It is mind that makes one a sinner and another a saint. Beware of it. Let it not be restless. Let it seek its Source, Life, or *Prana*, and merge itself therein. And let the *Prana* seek its origin and be in its turn assimilated in the great Void. Then only can the Peace that passeth all understanding be ushered in.

☆☆☆ OM TAT SAT OM ☆☆☆

51

THE VISION OF COMPLETENESS

In the Vision of completeness, overflowing with His bliss,
I'm complete, I'm perfect, in effulgent peace,
Radiant in happiness, full of serinity —
Na thasya karyam karanam cha vidyathe.

I have had the Vision. Times without number have I had it. In it I see everything as complete and perfect. There are no duties to be performed by me and those that have been performed are performed and finished for ever.

I am bubbling with laughter because of completeness. I am overflowing with happiness. So I see nothing else but to laugh and laugh.

It is a Vision of Perfection, of Completeness. There is nothing to be taken away from it, nothing to be added unto it. Once we possess this Vision there is nothing more to be done or undone. "*Na thasya karyam karanam cha vidyathe.*"

☆☆☆ OM TAT SAT OM ☆☆☆

52

WHY DON'T YOU LAUGH WHEN TROUBLES COME?

Why don't you laugh, when troubles come?
In trials, in tests, you never must moan.
There is but one sorrow, one trouble for the soul,
To lose God. The Real State—your only Goal!

Yesterday I received a blackmailing letter cavilling at me and the Ashram work. Yet shall I moan over it, shall I be depressed and cast down? Can the Sun of my Soul be affected by the passing clouds of praise and calumny? In His own unique splendour and glory He shines, clouds or no clouds.

This is now the proper time for me to laugh. When troubles and tribulations come, when tests and trials come, then is the time to laugh. In praises and laudations it is easy to find God. But that finding is not complete unless and until you find God in blame and calumny in failure and ignominy. Now therefore is the time for me to laugh and be happy. After all there can be only one real sorrow, one trouble for the Soul. And that is, when It forgets Its own nature. So long as It is aware of its own Real State and is firmly established in Itself, It can laugh at all imaginary troubles..

☆☆☆ OM TAT SAT OM ☆☆☆

53

PRAY FOR STRONGER SHOULDERS

Give me, O God, stronger shoulders
To bear all burden with a smile;
I'll never groan, I'll never murmur,
I'll drink the cup of your choice wine.

I know that I can bear my troubles,
I know that you will help your son.
And though your ways are quite mysterious,
Thy will, O Lord, it may be done!

The wise man never prays to God for lessening his burdens or removing them. He only prays for a stronger back so that he may bear all burdens with smiles. The weak and ignorant man when he is passing through fiery ordeals cries aloud, "Lord, do I deserve these?" Yes, he deserves them all. They are all intended. Not a straw moves without the Lord's command. All troubles and trials are there to test your fortitude and equanimity. Every new experience is for your own good. Any one can be spiritual when all is well. The acid test is on, only in the thick of troubles and misery. As such the wise mannever groans or murmurs. To the last he drains the cup that is set before him by his Lord, whether the cup be of choice wine or deadly poison.

Further the Lord never sends us troubles and sorrows that cannot be borne by us. He gives us only what each of us can bear and he gives them not to avenge upon us, but to put our mettle to test and enable our soul to grow. Incomprehensible and mysterious are God's ways. Peace belongs to him only who can say with all his heart, *"Not my will, O Lord, may Thine be done."*

☆☆☆ OM TAT SAT OM ☆☆☆

54

PEACE IS WITHIN

Do you seek Peace in symbols,
In temples, in masters, in friends?
Don't seek divine Peace outside,
For empty will be your heart.

The Peace you long for, is in you,
In the stillness of your won heart.
Steep in the inner silence,
Peace inside and outside, then you find.

Seekest thou Peace in symbols and shibboleths, in vain and empty things outside? Unprofitable is thy effort then. Peace, infinite peace, cannot be found in finite teachers. and masters, in cults and temples, in societies and friends?

The Peace for which you long is within you, in the stillness of your own purified heart. If you desire it, be still and give up relying on outside things. Arrest your restless mind and sink into the Silence within. When you are steeped in inner Peace, when you are soaked in it to the marrows of your bones, you will come to see it, not only within, but also without in the outside things also. Everywhere you will find it then. In fact you will be flooded with it from all sides.

☆☆☆ OM TAT SAT OM ☆☆☆

55

FEELING THE PRESENCE

How can I feel His Presence?
I long for it whatever I do.
Now hear: there is only One Power,
Expressing itself in you.

Be aware of the One Great Master.
Living in body and mind,
Think of Him, think of Him always,
And Him for ever you'll find.

Strange it may seem but every time I wash my hands and wipe them with a towel, I feel the interpenetrating Presence intensely. So at times I keep on drying my hands indefinitely. I do not know why I should feel His Presence especially in this motion of my hands. Probably the Freudians would come out with one of their queer explanations. Let them! But what is necessary for me is to try and feel the same experience in all that I do. For instance I am now writing. What is it that writes through this hand? What is it that thinks in my brain? It is the same One and Indivisible Power that is expressing Itself in all these motions. He is the Master of all motions. Let us be aware of His presence in all motions of the mind as well as in the body, in thoughts and deeds.

☆☆☆ OM TAT SAT OM ☆☆☆

56

INFINITE IN THE FINITE

Still I am bound to the body.
How long shall I bear this weight?
When its function gets fulfilled,
Then like a dry leaf will it fade.

O Glory, when the soul leaves the body,
In the Omnipresence to merge!
When the jug is for ever broken,
The infinite soul gets new birth.

I feel free and complete within. But this feeling is only inner, for it is still bound to the body, though it be an illusion. The Infinite within the finite is the idea that expresses my present feeling. Though this is not the highest state, the *Videha Kaivalya*, yet this state gives one peace and poise.

But how long can the Infinite be confined within the finite body? How long can the body bear the weight and immensity of the Infinite? When its function is fulfilled, like a dry leaf the body will drop off without effort. Then will the soul come out of the body and will completely merge within its own Omnipresence, Omnipotence and Omniscience. The ether enclosed within the jug becomes entirely one with the all-pervading ether if the jug is broken, though it was not different from it even before. These are mysteries known only to the knowers of the Soul.

☆☆☆ OM TAT SAT OM ☆☆☆

57

MOMENTS OF ELEVATION AND DEPRESSION

Don't sigh in moments of darkness,
When misery faces you.
Even wings of the mystics are tired,
When shadows of misery surround them.

But the saints shadows, realize they are
That come and pass and fade.
As the tortoise withdraws its limbs,
In the inner centre, saints wait.

In the inner centres abiding,
They wait till danger is past,
To soar high into the regions
Of rapture, now won at last.

Mystics and saints have soared high into the regions of the formless, in their moments of ecstasy and rapture. But they cannot stay there for ever. When their wings are tired, they come down, and they too have their moments of sadness and sorrow. In the face of cruelty, injustice, corruption and misery they too have their sufferings.

☆☆☆ OM TAT SAT OM ☆☆☆

Thus in every life there are moments of elevation and inspiration as well as moments of darkness and misery. But there is a difference between the sage and the man of the world. The sage looks at the phenomena of life perched on the pedestal of his soul-poise and equanimity. When misery and suffering face him, at once he realizes them as passing shadows which are worth not any attention. Quickly he withdraws himself into his own inner centre, the nucleus of his Soul and there he abides untouched by outward influence, like the tortoise which withdraws all its limbs into its shell in face of danger, and only comes out when that danger is past. "*Yatha samharate chayam kurmanganiva sarvasah.*"

AUM

I cannot afford to forget God or the self-effulgent Light, even for the fraction of a millionth of a second.

The man who has Cosmic Sense does not desire Eternal Life, for he has It.

The Holy Breath — Soham, kills egoism and destroys Ignorance and creates Love and Laughter in the heart and Peace in the Soul.

☆☆☆ OM TAT SAT OM ☆☆☆

58

WORK DRIVES AWAY ALL WORRY

Don't worry, dear soul, don't worry.
In reality all is joy.
For God, He gave you a servant,
That nothing may you annoy.

You know the name of this servant,
His noble name is Work
All worry will quickly fade,
That nothing, nothing can hurt.

Why feel sad and worried, my child? What is there to be worried over? What is worry? Where does it come from? If you analyse, it dwindles into nothing, for at the source all is light and joy.

Do you not remember the powerful saying, "**Work kills no one, But worry kills multitudes**." When you have grown blue with worry, begin to do some work, for work drives away all worry. After all, God is not yet dead. So long as He is alive, the Light and the Law remain. Why worry? Wake up and bask in the Light and follow the Law.

Worry is a terrible but only an imaginary vampire. Never give in, to this terrible mental melody. Where is this dark cloud of worry in the Sun of suns?

☆☆☆ OM TAT SAT OM ☆☆☆

59

HAPPINESS IS IN UNION WITH GOD

This will be my happiest day!
Say so, when greeting the sun.
Spend it in the Lord's service,
And as His godlike son.

Happiness lies in union
With God, the Indwelling Light.
In work as well as in silence,
Feel God's Presence — your day will be bright.

Wake up every day with a firm determination to make it the happiest and best day of your life. You can do so. It all lies in the way you make use of those tiny but precious moments, which make up the day. Spend them all in the Lord's service and in our absorption in Him.

Real happiness consists not in the possession of many cattle, elephants and horses, automobiles and gold, beautiful damsels and houses.. *(Bahun pasun hasthi hiranyam asvan...Ramah saradhah sa turyah.)* It lies only in union with God, the Indwelling light. As man tries to feel oneness with the Light within, and that which is also without, he becomes happy and contented whether he is working or meditating. To feel God's Presence in both work and silence, moment by moment — that is the way to make this day the best as well as the happiest.

☆☆☆ OM TAT SAT OM ☆☆☆

60

THE REAL ADJUSTMENT IS WITHIN

All adjustment must start from within,
From the source of peace in your heart.
Don't think of reforming others,
To adjust Yourself be your part!

Man wants to adjust, rearrange and remake everything in the outside world. But he does not try to adjust himself. Yet the real adjustment, the real orientation should begin with himself, from within. When there is adjustment within, there is adjustment without. When there is Peace within, in the heart, all is Peace without also. Hence all adjustment and arrangement must start from within.

But, alas, the man of the world, when there is something wrong, wants to adjust everything else except himself. He tries to reform this man and that man, but lo, he has not yet reformed himself. He drops a letter to this man, he puts in a word to that man, trying to smooth things over and adjust them. But he does not go to the Source and does not adjust himself. If the individual wants Peace he must first adjust himself, reorientate himself, and this endeavour should begin from within.

☆☆☆ OM TAT SAT OM ☆☆☆

61

MAN IS A LION, BY NATURE

Man is the living image of God,
By his nature a lion, brave, keen on his road,
But trying with the things of the world of Maya,
He forgets his birthright, forgets Ananda.

Misery, agony, suffering and pain
Torture him now, again and again.
But the remedy is easy and always at hand:
Renounce false desires, come to your own land.

Man, the living image of God, is by his very nature a lion. His birthright is to tear away the veils of ignorance. But due to wrong association and false imaginations he has forgotten to roar and has learnt to bleat. He quakes with fear at every turn of mind. Facts have been reversed. Man, the image of the Highest, has forgotten his intrinsic nature and has become a fool trying with the goods of the world.

As a result, man has become subject to misery, agony, suffering and untold physical and mental suffering. If he gives up identifying himself with the body, and renounces his false fears and desires, he will come into his own. He will be then installed in his real status and stature.

☆☆☆ OM TAT SAT OM ☆☆☆

62

IMAGINATION A MERE REED

Sometimes there is on your onward march
A reed of false thoughts, that hinders your start.
Crush it and trample it under your feet,
Burn it away with the fire of God.

Burn it away with His holy fire,
And burn now away your wrong desire;
Be not a prey to the things of the world,
Recognize the Reality, the Absolute Word.

Will you allow a mere reed, the reed of wrong and false imagination, to obstruct your Onward March? Or will you trample on and crush this insignificant reed under your foot and burn it away in all-consuming fire of God-consciousness?

It is high time to assert and express the Highest in you. Do not become a prey to false appearances and wrong imaginations. Recognize the Reality, the Absolute and be established in THAT.

☆☆☆ OM TAT SAT OM ☆☆☆

63

AFRAID OF SHADOWS

Be rooted in a firm, indestructable rock,
Don't look at the shadows, they are but fog.
Brahman is in you and Thou art That.
Passing storms and onslaughts, like shadows,
will fade.

In spite of all religions and philosophies, and inspite of the repetitions of the sacred vedic texts like "I am Brahman," "Thou art that," etc., the learned man is still afraid of shadows of the world — sorrows and fears. Why? Because he has not had a personal experience of the Truth, in daily life.

Often it is a philosopher or a priest who succumbs to the passing trifle. All this is because he does not stand on a secure foundation. If you are rooted in a firm, deep and rocky foundation, you will withstand the onslaughts of all the passing storms of lust, fear and ignorance.

☆☆☆ OM TAT SAT OM ☆☆☆

64

GOOD LUCK

Good Luck! say so many, good luck indeed!
But my soul's luck itself, what else does it need!
Realizers of God — they have everything,
Having luck in themselves — His praise they sing.

I have on my table a Christmas greeting card with a picture of a black cat, wishing Good Luck. The cat's eyes are fixed with two glass beads and for its tail it has some fluffy stuff. Every time I glance at it, I read "GOOD LUCK". Good Luck, indeed! Is not my Soul itself Good Luck? What other luck or fortune does the Soul need?

The knowers of Self, the realizers of God need no Good Luck. They are themselves Good Luck. Their integral experience of the Divine is their Good Luck. In it they have everything.

☆☆☆ OM TAT SAT OM ☆☆☆

65

MAKE THE BLESSED MOMENT PERMANENT

There are moments when we feel His presence everywhere.
But where this state fades, you must not despair.
Merge in yourself, see the one Reality.
It's Light is everlasting — in all eternity!

There are moments when I feel the Presence, within, without, every where. I feel not only filled and surrounded by It, I feel completely saturated with It.

But this Presence is not something which is transitory and momentary. It is permanent and everlasting, but somehow due to an illusion, man forgets It and becomes desolate. But when there is only one Reality, the Light of lights, and when there is nothing else besides, whence does the illusion come? That is the mystery, the illusiveness of the illusion, the *maya*. But if man merges within himself and ponders deeply, he will see that the illusion is not based on anything, that it is devoid of any substance and that in fact there is no illusion, as ALL IS LIGHT.

☆☆☆ OM TAT SAT OM ☆☆☆

66

I CANNOT FORGET MY SELF

I can and I may forget anything,
My self can't be forgotten, nor can I forget Him.
For God and myself both always are one.
The One without a Second as the ray and the sun

With vividness I have realised another facet of Truth this time. I have had the Vision again. Of what is the Vision this time? It is of the truth that I cannot forget MY SELF. I can and may forget anything. But how can I forget Myself? And in as much as I remember MY SELF — I remember the Eternal and the Real, for I am the Real and the Eternal.

That which thinks in me is that very Self. Of course not all its glory is expressed either in thought or action. But yet how can I forget it? I can forget those who love me and those who differ from me, but certainly I cannot forget MY SELF, the One without a Second.

☆☆☆ OM TAT SAT OM ☆☆☆

67

VISION UNIVERSAL

All is God, all is the One Self alone.
The whole world is included — a new truth I have
won!
The waves of the ocean, they are all the same,
They had but one source and had but one aim.

And all mankind is part of God, the Divine,
They all have a soul, holy, sublime.
I long to embrace all whether evil or good,
They are countless waves of spiritual floods.

In this new Vision, I have no more any enemies or rivels. I see no tormentors or persecutors. MY SELF — All is God, the One SELF. No one, nothing is excluded from this Vision. All are included in it, for the entire world is only a component of it.

I long to embrace all, not only those who love me, but those who cannot love me, not only these who are good and holy, but also those who are ugly and cruel. For verily, they are all aspects of the Divine. They are the countless waves of one and the same Ocean. Let all the vibrations merge into the One and Indivisible Source of all.

☆☆☆ OM TAT SAT OM ☆☆☆

68

LIGHT IS FREE OF FINITE PLANS

I am the Light, the resplendent Light,
The Eternal, Effulgent and Infinite Light.
Time has vanished, and action will cease.
All homage be to that splendour of Bliss!

Above space, above time the same Light for ever,
It remains as it is, decreases never.
It shines on all, that splendour of Peace.
All homage be to that splendour of Bliss!

I am the Light, the effulgent and resplendent Light. The Eternal and Infinite Light. What are my plans? None. Time vanishes in this ALL-LIGHT. Action ceases in this all accomplished Light.

The Light remains as Light, it decreases not, neither does it increase. It shines equally on all, under all conditions. It is the same Light which is for ever. It is above space, time and causation. All homage be unto that Splendour of splendours, the *All-Light!*

☆☆☆ OM TAT SAT OM ☆☆☆

69

GOOD FRIDAY — THE SINGING BIRDS

To day is Good Friday, most sacred a day
To all who follow the Lord's holy way.
The birds are singing their joyful song,
And lilies are blooming the way all along.

Today is Good Friday, the day most blessed and sacred to all Christians. But who is a Christian? All those who follow the way of the Lord. From early dawn, today, the birds have been singing and singing — birds of all species, sizes and plumage.

They want me to join them in singing the praises of the Lord. But I cannot, this being the thirty-eighth day of my silent Fast. For the next two days I can only sing within myself. And then, I too shall break into song, as do these birds, praising the Good Lord for all His Blessings.

Easter is associated with Lilies. In the West they call them Easter Lilies. All through the Ashrama, hundreds of lilies are coming out of their sheaths and are laying bare their hearts, greeting and welcoming the Christ Resurrected.

☆☆☆ OM TAT SAT OM ☆☆☆

70

BLESSED EASTER

All is greeting the Resurrected Christ!
His praise will rise from the earth to the skies.
He is in the Light, ever present is He,
A witness of life in eternity.

In memory of the Blessed Easter, the Good Friday, I long to express Him, in each and every moment of my life. No more forgetting of Him, no more the illusion. Within and without is He present as the Light of Lights. In silence and work, in every moment of my mind and body, it is He who is expressing Himself. Not only in the waking state, but in dream and sleep also is the Light present as the silent Witness of all phenomena.

☆☆☆ OM TAT SAT OM ☆☆☆

71

GOD HAS NO OTHER BODY ON EARTH EXCEPT YOURS

God has no body except yours on earth.
He's thinking in your mind ever since your birth.
He's sparkling in your eye and listening in your ear.
His Light is your light, you have nothing to fear.

God has no other body on earth except yours. He has no other hands except yours. He has no other legs or feet except yours. Verily, He is thinking in your mind, sparkling in your eyes, listening in your ears and flowing in your breath. His face is your face. His love is your Love. His Light is your Light. Now, He has taken possession of your body completely, more than ever, with His Light, Life and Love. The old self of fear and self-defence is dead because God, the Spirit of Peace, Love and Light possesses the body now and will possess it for ever.

☆☆☆ OM TAT SAT OM ☆☆☆

72

THE RISEN CHRIST

Ascension Day of the Risen Christ!
Myself dead and buried; could I live in his light!
And lo! my new Self lives, breathes in Him,
All homage to the Master, the holiest King!

In memory of the Good Friday, how my soul longs to say that Swami Omkar's body, the physical sheath is dead, and buried too, and that the Blessed Spirit of Christ has risen from this tomb of oblivion or darkness!

It is wonderful to allow the old self to die and get buried and to express the New Self or the Higher Self, the Spirit of Christ, to shine ceaselessly. It is a comfort and consolation that the Christ-spirit works, lives, breathes in future, through and in this form. Let the Christ spirit express itself in future in little things as well as in big things, even in the daily acts of seeing, hearing, thinking, writing etc.

May all homage be unto the Risen Christ on this Holy Ascension Day, and may we meditate now, on His innocent Face of beauty, purity, compassion and Peace!

☆☆☆ OM TAT SAT OM ☆☆☆

73

LOVE GOD FOR THE SAKE OF LOVE

Do you seek God to get rid of your pain?
To be free from your trials — and forget Him again?
And remember Him only when fresh troubles arise?
You think of your ego alone, that's not wise.

My child, you must long for Him with all your heart,
He must be your all-in-all, being His part.
Apart from Him all is darkness and death,
So love God for His sake who's your life and your breath.

My child, do you want God, because He is your Life, Soul, Goal and your all-in-all? Or do you wish to love Him as temporary palliative to get rid of your troubles and passing clouds? If you are longing to have God or to realise God, only to be free from the tests, trials, and tribulations of your daily life, as soon as those passing clouds pass away or disappear, you will forget God, you will leave Him aside again. And you will remember Him again only when some fresh trouble arises.

Oh my child, it is high time to learn to love God for the sake of love; and to work, breathe and live for Him, because He is the Breath of your breath, the Life of your life and the Soul of your soul. Apart from Him all else is chaos, darkness and death. So LOVE GOD, FOR THE SAKE OF GOD ONLY!

☆☆☆ OM TAT SAT OM ☆☆☆

74

BE ABOVE PRAISE AND BLAME

When you are flattered and praised in a speech,
Don't feel like a child, that gets a few sweets.
You even forget God again and again
For some praise of the world that dies like a flame

And when you are worried and when you earn blame,
Don't waste time and life, the fault is the same.
Rise above duality of every kind,
Be above praise and blame, waveless in mind.

Worldly men are like little children. When children get a few sweets they are happy. When they get a few bumps and knocks they weep. When a letter comes praising and flattering them, offering sympathy and help, man is besides himself with great joy. He forgets even God, the Indwelling Light and begins to think and rejoice over the words of the sympathy again and again, for days to come.

Again when he gets a cruel letter, a letter of criticism and condemnation he begins to worry and waste his precious time and life, not only for days but for months, thinking over the cruel thrusts and unwarranted and undeserving remarks. A wise man should be above praise and blame. Another helpful way to bear the blame is, when you feel sad, remember all the good that you get also, and thus overcome the sorrow with joy, the evil with good. Peace belongs to those who have risen above duality of every kind.

☆☆☆ OM TAT SAT OM ☆☆☆

75

LOVE GOD SELFLESSLY

Don't seek God for help in your troubles only!
He is present with you eternally,
Pervading, permeating the very cells of us all.
There is no separation, hear on His call.

Do you want God for the sake of Love, because He is all Love? Or do you want Him to help you to smooth over and adjust your troubles in your life? If you want god for the sake of Love or Truth without expecting any reward behold, He is already within you pervading and permeating the very cells of your being. He is eternally present with you from eternity to eternity. There is never a moment of separation between God and yourself.

If you want God for the sake of removing your troubles or granting boons, I do not know, where He is. Go to those people who are in troubles, seeking God only because of their troubles. They will direct you to their God, who is in the far away Heaven, only to serve them, granting them health, plenty of wealth and the other goods of the world as well as a long life in which to enjoy them.

Dear one, if you long to have God, for the sake of love, then come to me. Behold! He is with you, nay in you NOW AND ALWAYS.

☆☆☆ OM TAT SAT OM ☆☆☆

76

ALL COMES FROM WITHIN

The flower comes from the plant and the plant from the seed,
The thought creates the word and the word the deed.
All comes from within, from one same source,
From Creative Silence, the one Great Cause.

Everything comes from within. This Ashrama, this world, all thinking and writing comes from Within. All sound and all work are from the Silence, all form and colour from the Formless. What you have thought, spoken or done has all come from Within. What you are aiming to think, speak or do in the future also, is going to come from the same source, the great Silence, The bubble comes from the wave and the wave comes from the Ocean.

The flower comes from the bud and the bud comes from the plant. The deed comes from the word, the word comes from the thought and the thought comes from the Source, from Within. Let everything, every manifestation merge Within, in the Great Beyond, to attain the Final, Freedom or the Infinite Peace.

☆☆☆ OM TAT SAT OM ☆☆☆

77

EVERY MOMENT IS PRECIOUS

I long to feel His Presence, the Indwelling Light,
I long to feel It by day and by night.
Every moment is precious, when spent in Him,
Who is within and without, His Glory we sing!

I long to feel the Presence, the Interpenetrating Presence more than ever, rather than wasting precious time in writing these pages. But as long as I am feeling the Presence now, how can I be wasting the precious TIME! There is not a moment of waste, so long as one is centred in THAT, the only Reality, the Indwelling Light. It does everything in activity as well as in Silence.

Anyway, as this is the Fortieth Day of the Fast, I feel every moment is precious more than ever. How am I going to spend this last day of the Fast? Of course the day will be spent only in feeling the Presence, within and without, in recognizing the Presence, in me, as well as in others, even in the so-called foes, the ignorant children of the One God. Glory be unto Thee O Lord! within, without, above, below and all around, on every side and in every form!

☆☆☆ OM TAT SAT OM ☆☆☆

78

EASTER SUNDAY

Easter, the holiest day for all followers of Christ
Of all Masters of mankind He is the most wise.
He is in my soul, in my body too,
The Holy Master in me and in you.

Today is Easter SUNDAY, the Holiest Day for all the Christians, nay for all lovers and devoted followers of the Blessed Christ. It is a wonderful unexpected coincidence, as it was not calculated or thought of, that this sacred Easter Sunday should be the last day of my Fast of Forty Days.

Today more than ever, that great thought, that **Christ has no other body on earth than mine**, is prominent in my thoughts and feelings. Is not this one inspiring and Soul-awakening thought enough for all my penance of fasting or feasting in these forty days? I gaze and gaze today, even outwardly at the Holy Statue and pictures of Blessed Christ to see whether there are any changes or similar features in the physical body too. Yet, my one joy, consolation and strength is that the Spirit that was in Christ is in me also. And it is in you too, eternally.

☆☆☆ OM TAT SAT OM ☆☆☆

79

DO NOT COMPLAIN

If you desire to be one with God,
You must not complain.
No test and no sorrow shall separate you from Him,
Or your strife is in vain.

If crushed and tormented in body and mind,
Hold fast to the Lord!
Do not complain in death nor in life.
God is your part.

"**If you desire to be one with God, do not complain. If you do complain you cannot be one with Him**." Today I came across these wise words uttered in his tests and trials by a Muslim Saint. This is the last examination in God-identification. If a man puts both his hands around your throat to choke your life out of you, you are to see only the sweet face of God in him. If a man gives you a fond embrace with one hand, and with the other hand stabs you in the back, you are to feel God's Presence in the very touch of his hand.

Then alone will the latent Light in you manifest in all Glory. The saints and sages have done it in the past. They never complained of their tests and tribulations. Here is a chance for you too, to recognize God. When others have done it, why can't you do it? Do it now and be a blessing to the world of humanity.

☆☆☆ OM TAT SAT OM ☆☆☆

80

SILENCE IS GOLD AND SPEECH IS SILVER

Silence is gold, and speech is silver.
How true is this saying!
There is power in silence, as great souls know,
But speech can hurt.

If speaking, speak with sweetness
And love at every hour;
And your thoughts be as flashes of lightning of peace
And your words — thunderbolts of power!

Since the last forty days I have not been speaking. Tonight ends the Silent Feast of Forty Days. Tomorrow begins the day of my speech, the life of hustling and bustling again. Yet, I wish to speak only when most necessary and be silent for the rest of the time. When I speak I love to see my words filled with sweetness, love, compassion and forgiveness. They should be the thunderbolts of Power and Illumination, but not of destruction and death.

I love to have my thoughts also as flashes of lightning. Indeed, there is power in Silence. How true are the words: Silence is gold and speech is silver! All great souls who ever did any good to the world, have been of few words. Let the words be the thunderbolts of Power. Let the thoughts be the Lightnings of Peace and Illumination!

☆☆☆ OM TAT SAT OM ☆☆☆

81

SELF-RELIANCE

Rely on yourself and on nobody else,
And happy you will ever be.
You are the Eternal and Infinite Self.
Self-reliance makes you free.

Self-reliance and self-radiance, has been the living message of all seers and saints, in both the East and the West. Religion begins with Self-reliance and ends in Self-realization. Self-Reliance in the beginning, middle and end is real life. What is life without Self-reliance, except a bundle of fears, sorrows and maladies.

The man of Self-reliance is the happiest man, for he relies on no one else, but on Himself, for his Happiness and Peace. If there is strength anywhere, it is only in Self-reliance, when a man realizes that he is the Eternal and Infinite Self, which is within, without and all pervading.

☆☆☆ OM TAT SAT OM ☆☆☆

82

HE WHO ADMITS DEFEAT, IS BEATEN

He only is beaten, who admits defeat.
Are'nt you the Image of God!
How can you be helpless, how can you feel weak,
In sad and sorrowful mood?

Feel oneness with Him, the Indwelling Light,
Though crushed and alone,
You've nothing to fear, there's no cause for fright
And you have won.

He only is beaten who admits it. What is that "it"? It is the defeat or weakness. Why should man, being the living Image of God, admit any weakness or defeat? When he feels his oneness with God, his Creator, how can he admit any sickness or weakness? How can he be helpless and soulless, being the very *Atman*, the Soul of souls.

So long as we do not deny the Indwelling Light, there is no need to admit any defeat, even when crushed and trodden under the heels of the oppressor or persecutor. As Soul, the powerful *Atman*, you have nothing but power of Omnipresence, Omnipotence and Omniscience. Hence, you are always the Witness, in spite of the ups and downs of life.

☆☆☆ OM TAT SAT OM ☆☆☆

83

SUNRISE FROM WITHIN

See the sun coming with his glimmering light,
Spreading his splendour after dark night.
So we are filled with the Light from within,
Self-shining in our soul, in eternal spring.

I often wait for the Sunrise. It is interesting to see the glimmering light, slowly and silently filling the universe with Light. Today, I had to wait long, to see the Sun coming out of the horizon. Then the thought came: Why wait for this outer Sun, the light of the world to come out, when there is already the Sun of suns within you, eternally present, only awaiting your recognition **Now**, in the living present moment.

He who relies on the Sun of suns within, need not wait for the outer sun to come out. He is ever filled with the self-shining Light of the Soul, which is One without a second.

☆☆☆ OM TAT SAT OM ☆☆☆

84

ONENESS WITH NATURE

Look at the trees and the sweet smelling flowers,
Feel their fragrance of love.
Listen to the birds, gaze at the mountains
And the twinkling stars from above.

I am one with Nature, the mirror of God;
With her beauty I am one.
Don't worry if others turn against you,
Pay homage to Nature alone.

As I gaze at the tall trees, the little shrubs and the climbing creepers, I feel so happy at their oneness and sympathy. I feel the fragrance of love in their sweet-smelling flowers. As I listen to the soft, musical notes of the birds, I feel happy at their love and companionship. As I look around and face the blue mountains, I feel strength, from their firmness. Again, as I look up at the sky at night-fall into the shining face of twinkling stars, I sense their kindred relationship with me.

When all these are my own, what even if one ignorant, selfish and arrogant man turns against me? It is weakness and ignorance to see anything other than God. Nature pays homage to the one who loves Nature. Blessed are the lovers of Nature! Verily, all this is God!

☆☆☆ OM TAT SAT OM ☆☆☆

85

WHO IS THE RICHEST MAN?

The richest is he who uses the moments,
The precious moments out of price.
He is fearless and powerful, never weak or frail,
Living as in a paradise.

I long to be the Richest Man in all the world, by making the best use of these tiny, precious little moments, which contain in their heart, Omnipresence, Omnipotence and Omniscience.

What I have will grow only by being used in the best possible way. Let me not waste this great wealth, the priceless moments by squandering them for the sake of anything. The Richest Man is the most Powerful Man too. The most Powerful Man is the most Fearless Man too. Unto such belongs the Kingdom of Heaven and the Paradise of Peace but never to the frail creature of fear, weakness and poverty of heart.

May we ever become the Richest, by making the best use of our precious moments!

☆☆☆ OM TAT SAT OM ☆☆☆

86

THE FAST IS COMPLETE

The Fast is complete, the feast at an end,
Glory be to our God!
The work is done and peace is won,
Glory be to our God!

Freedom, atlast! The Fast is complete and the Feast has ended. The naked were clothed and the Poor were fed in memory of the happy ending of the fast, glorifying God, for all His richest blessings. In the Ashram we had special prayers and meditations. One devoted Brother came all the way from Madras, to help in the function and he presided over the meeting.

I was asked to speak, for the first time after forty days of silence. Alas! words did not come but tears of ecstasy began to flow. When I attempted to speak, my voice was hoarse and very weak. I could hardly speak. God has been very good to me in every way helping in the happy consummation of the Fast, through all these devoted souls who have come from far and near. May God bless them all and bless you all too!

☆☆☆ OM TAT SAT OM ☆☆☆

87

EXAGGERATION

Let us not exaggerate, though it is not a crime;
In all you say, be correct.
Little things can teach us, as well as the big.
Strive to be always correct.

Exaggeration is not considered as a mistake. We allow it to pass on as a common occurrence. It is the every day life of the average man. Yet, although it is not a crime, it is a blemish and lie too. In one of my Messages in Telugu written during the fast, I have written that a Lemon tree which is near the bathroom, is trying to help me, by giving out nearly ten lemons in this summer season, when lemons are scarce.

Everyday whenever I see the tree, the question comes — "Did you not exaggerate the number of lemons? " Then, I began to count 1, 2, 3, 4, 5. Perhaps, there are not ten lemons. There may be less lemons. Thus, I keep on counting unconsciously every day. As the tree is full of leaves, the lemons are hidden in the leaves.

Anyway for the Peace of my Soul, to be more exact and correct, I have changed the number of lemons in the message from ten to five. Thus, one can improve and grow in little things as well as in big things.

☆☆☆ OM TAT SAT OM ☆☆☆

88

HISTORY REPEATS ITSELF

The Law of sowing and reaping
Will always be the same.
History repeats itself,
Always, again and again.

Like Christ on the cross, amidst soldiers.
Hard-hearted and cruel they were,
So innocent people must suffer too
By cruelty everywhere.

But though the wicked are laughing
When seeming success they have won,
The law of sowing and reaping
Will protect or spare no one.

Often these days, the picture of Christ on the Cross and the hard-hearted and cruel soldiers, playing cards, drinking and swearing, sitting at the foot of the cross comes before my vision. It seems they also were casting lots, as to who should own the Robe that was worn by the Blessed Christ. The terrible, heart-renting and agonising crucifixion was all a big fun to them.

How many similar tragedies have been enacted even in the present times on innocent people, by men of arrogance, selfishness and ignorance. They feel so self satisfied over their seeming success in persecuting innocent ones. But do they ever think of the future of the Roman soldiers who crucified Christ?

History tells us that of the cruel soldiers who crucified Christ, one committed suicide, another became mad and the lives of those others too ended in disgrace. Let the persecutors of the innocent, the Modern Roman Soldiers laughing at their seeming success, be aware of their future which does not protect or spare anyone, but all have to fulfil the law of sowing and reaping!

ASHTAVAKRA SAYS

My Child! Yet may often speak up on various scriptures or hear them. But you cannot be established in the Self unless you forget all.

All are unhappy because they exert themselves, but none knows this. The blessed one attains emancipation through SELF.

Happiness belongs to that master idler to whom even the closing and opening of eyelids is an affliction, to none else.

Having known yourself to be THAT in which the universe appears like waves on the sea, why do you run about like a miserable being?

Completely give up even contemplation and hold nothing in your mind. You are verily the SELF and therefore free. What will you gain by thinking?

☆☆☆ OM TAT SAT OM ☆☆☆

89

GOD ALONE NEVER DISAPPOINTS

Rely on nobody else,
Disappointed you always will be.
Therefore don't trust on others,
Disappointments you always will see.

There is only One to be trusted,
Our God, by day and by night.
However delusive be Maya
Trust but the Indwelling Light!

The world is full of disappointments. Often the one whom you trust and consider as your own, fails to stand by you in your great test. There is only ONE, who is your own, which is God, the Higher-Self. So long as you rely on frail man, who is easily influenced by others, you will have not one disappointment, but a hundred, thousand, nay a million disappointments.

Man, however devoted he may be, disappoints us, but there is only One, who cannot disappoint us. That one is the God within, the Invisible Self. How thick and delusive is *Maya*, that makes even the wise rely on the outer man, rather than on the Indwelling Light! Let all disappointments, the stumbling blocks be made into stepping stones!

☆☆☆ OM TAT SAT OM ☆☆☆

90

INFINITE POWER IS WITHIN YOU

O Man, child of God, wake up
From your slumber full of fear;
Infinite power is within you,
All darkness will disappear.

All darkness will disappear;
Be not frightened by the ocean of life.
Assert your strength and your power,
Be a hero in struggle and strife.

There is an interesting story about the fight, between a little fish and the mighty Ocean. It seems the ocean was quivering and shivering with fear, because a little fish from its bosom wanted to bully and fight with the ocean.

Such has been the miserable plight and shameful condition of many a man in the world. Being the Unlimited Ocean of Power, he quakes and fears, at the opposition of a little insignificant fish, in the ocean of life.

O! Man, child of God, not only one little fish, but even a million fish in the ocean can never mar, touch or change your dignity or equilibrium. Wake up, from your deep slumbers of ignorance and darkness and assert your strength and thus quell the struggles of all the fish in the world.

☆☆☆ OM TAT SAT OM ☆☆☆

91

I AM THE RICHEST MAN

Looking at the rising sun
I feel as the richest man,
Inhaling, exhaling God,
Breathing His holy name.

I am the richest man,
Most powerful, fearless too,
I am the Infinite Light,
Glory and Silence anew.

It was my first descent to the foot of the Hill after the Fast of Forty Days. The Sun was just coming up from the horizon and I could not be confined to closed doors. I felt like going out and began to walk in the rays of the rising Sun, feeling the Presence then. At the foot of the hill sitting on a small rock, I was looking into the Soul of the sun. That was one of the sacred moments, when I felt that I was the richest man in all the world.

Unconsciously, I was meditating on the Breath repeating the following affirmation:

☆☆☆ OM TAT SAT OM ☆☆☆

I am the richest man in the world, with this Breath.

I am the most powerful man in the world, with the second Breath.

I am the most fearless man in the world, with the third Breath.

And with the fourth Breath, I am the Indivisible Light, the One without a second.

It was Light, within, without, above and below. What else can be said of that Infinite Light? Glory! Peace and Silence!

☆☆☆ OM TAT SAT OM ☆☆☆

92

QUARREL OF BIRDS WITH OCEAN

Two birds were quarrelling with the ocean,
That had washed away their egg.
"We shall dry up all your waters,
If you do'nt give it back!"

Drop by drop they carried the waters,
Till the ocean returned the egg.
With patience you will be winning
Your aim, in whatever you lack.

There is another really interesting story about a quarrel of a pair of little birds with the powerful ocean. It seems the female bird was laying its eggs in the sands of the sea within the reach of ebb and flow of the tide. The eggs were getting washed away by the waves of the ocean. So, the little birds became furious with the ocean and declared war on it. They said, if their eggs were not returned to them, they would dry up the waters of the ocean. The ocean smiled and murmured "Go Ahead, with all your might."

The little birds, began to carry the water from the ocean in their tiny beaks and empty it on the land. The story goes on to tell us that all the other birds joined in their good cause because of their right cause and even the king of birds, Garuda, joined them. The ocean then got afraid and returned their tiny eggs with an apology. Such should be the patience to realise the Goal of Life. Success always belongs to the just, the patient and the righteous.

☆ ☆ ☆ OM TAT SAT OM ☆ ☆ ☆

93

THE POWER OF THOUGHT

What you are, comes out of your thoughts.
God if you think of, God you will be,
Dust if you think of, dust you are.
Watch your thoughts and you'll be free.

Blessed is the one, who is witness of his thoughts,
Twice blessed is the one, who is master of his mind,
Thrice blessed is the one, who has risen over all,
The kingdom of Heaven, thus will he find.

Since the dawn of creation, the power of thought has been scientifically proved. What you are, is the result of your thought. Thoughts are things. You will become what you think. Hence, it has been said by sages: **God if you think of, God you are! Dust if you think of, Dust you are!**

Constructive thinking leads to Peace, Power and Poise. Negative thinking leads to misery, agony, destruction and death. Hence, one should watch his thoughts.

Blessed is the one, who is the witness of his thoughts!

☆☆☆ OM TAT SAT OM ☆☆☆

Twice blessed is the one who is the master of his thoughts!

Thrice blessed is the one who has risen above thoughts!

Unto such belongs the Kingdom of Heaven. They alone know what that Peace that passeth all understanding is, but not the slaves of thought. Verily, **Man is the Master of His Own Destiny.**

☆☆☆ OM TAT SAT OM ☆☆☆

94

THE LITTLE TEMPEST

A great tempest had been at the death of Christ,
Filling the world with darkness and thunder.
A little tempest last Good Friday broke out;
Was it to remind us of the master's wonders?

It is said history repeats itself. The course of things that happened centuries ago is bound to happen again. Two thousand years ago at the time of the crucifixion of the Lord, the Bible tells us that there was a great tempest, shaking the buildings, uprooting the trees, filling the world with dread, darkness and chaos. The skies were vibrating with thunder and lightning.

Were the elements expressing their protest and sorrow over the innocent death of the Holiest and the most Innocent Person, the Son of God? Unbelievable and strange as it may sound, there was a little tempest, in a miniature scale, with thunder and lightning, after the recent Good Friday during my last Fast. The Mysteries of the Creator are known only to the Mystics.

☆☆☆ OM TAT SAT OM ☆☆☆

95

LEMON TREE

I had watered my lemon tree before my house,
Sweet smelling blossoms it bore, so white.
And one day it dropped one ripe lemon on the earth,
A sign of its gratitude, full of delight.

There is a lemon tree, that I have been taking care of, since the last forty days by allowing water to flow towards it, day after day, from the bath-room. It has been so greatful that now, that it is full of tender leaves and sweet smelling white blossoms, as if to help me in the fast, in these days when lemons are scarce, it has yielded nearly six lemons.

Everyday I was looking at them, for they were not yet ripe. The fast was getting almost finished. As if the lemon tree wanted that I should use one of its lemons at least, on a certain day in the fast it dropped on earth one ripe lemon, when I was in need of it. As I drank the juice of the lemon, the tree seems to be satisfied and I too felt satisfied, and grateful too. Gratitude is the thing that cements and unites the hearts of trees, animals and men.

☆ ☆ ☆ OM TAT SAT OM ☆ ☆ ☆

96

ATTACHMENT TO INANIMATE OBJECTS

Strange it may sound, we can get attached
To a place, to a room with its walls.
Lo, I spent hours of silence so deep
In meditation in a prayer hall.

And never I shall forget this time,
Communing in this little hall.
It gave me help and gave me love,
I feel grateful, grateful for all.

As I lie down in the Prayer Hall of *Sushila Mandir*, where I had the opportunity of spending the Forty Days Fast in prayer, meditation and silence, often and often my eyes look and look at the very walls and ceiling, lovingly. By staying too long at one place, it is strange how we get attached even to inanimate things. Often, I express my gratitude to this Prayer Hall, for providing this blessed opportunity of fasting in silence, communing with the Indwelling Presence.

Strange as it may sound, often with the following thoughts, I commune with the Prayer Hall: — "As I am going out now into the world of activity, after enjoying your company all these days, when will I see you again? Will I ever see you? As the body is unreal, who can tell of the morrow? Even if I do not have the chance to see you, I feel so deeply grateful to you, for all your help, sympathy and love."

☆☆☆ OM TAT SAT OM ☆☆☆

97

THE TWO SACRED BIRDS

A bird was singing in our hills,
Longing for all its beloved:
Where are you, my darling, where may you be,
At the beach, in the forest above?

The sweet longing cry was heard for hours.
And lo! the answer came:
The beloved is within you, in your own pure heart,
Shining so bright as a flame.

There are a pair of sweet birds in Totapalli Hills. We used to see them and hear their sweet songs at the time of the mango-season. The name of the bird is PIPPIHA. The song of the bird is 'PIU KAHAN', Piu means 'Beloved', Kahan means 'where is.' Where is the Beloved, is the note of those birds.

The heart-rending cry of those birds cannot be described in words. You ought to listen with your own ears as the bird repeats in pathos, hour after hour, seeking its Beloved with one deep resonant cry of PIU KAHAN: Where is the Beloved? Where is the sweet Beloved?

Somewhere from the distant hills, from the very great void, the answer comes in all stillness saying "THE BELOVED IS WITHIN, in the stillness of your own purified heart."

☆☆☆ OM TAT SAT OM ☆☆☆

98

GOD IS BOTH ACTIVE AND INACTIVE

God is active and inactive too,
In the unseen as well as the seen.
Adoration be to the Highest one,
Adoration and glory to Him!

God is both active and inactive. The Man of Wisdom says: **God does nothing**. The Man of Action says: **God does everything**. Who is right? Both of them are right, from their particular angle of view and understanding. In GITA, the Song Celestial, the Lord says that there are two states or conditions in the Spiritual Plane: the Unmanifested and the Manifested. Sri. Krishna continues to say in GITA that it is difficult to comprehend the Incomprehensible even for the Wise. But it is not so with the manifested. As the manifested is with form and name, any layman can comprehend and meditate on it.

But alas, man in his grossness due to *Maya*, because of the false identification with body, the bundle of blood and flesh, is ignoring and denying both the manifested and unmanifested in his daily life. Therefore Peace

Profound and Eternal belongs only to those rare and precious souls who can recognize the same Indivisible Light, both in the manifested, the seen, and in the unmanifested, the Unseen.

Verily, **God does everything**, for He is all-in-all and ever Complete — the One without a second. May our Adoration be unto the Unmanifested through the Manifested!

☆☆☆ OM TAT SAT OM ☆☆☆

99

MY THUNDERS AND LIGHTNINGS

When you speak, let your words be like thunders,
And your thoughts be like flame.
So I pondered, walking to and fro,
Seeing that a thunderstorm came.

In the thunders I heard my very own words,
And the lightnings were as my thoughts.
I felt God's Presence sacred and clear,
That thunders and lightnings had brought.

In one of the previous pages I have written thus: "*Since I was observing silence for forty days, when I speak this time, my words should be like thunderbolts and my thoughts should be like lightning.*"

One evening, I was walking to and fro on the terrace of the Mandir, striving to feel the Presence, with each and every step. The sky was cloudy and dark. There were signs of Thundering and Lightning in the sky.

Of course whenever there is thunder, there is the lightning also. But here comes the interesting part. Whenever I heard the thundering sounds, I was unconsciously saying to myself that those thunders were my words. Whenever there was the lightning I was repeating within, that this was my thought. How blessed it is to make the thunders and lightnings our words and thoughts!

☆☆☆ OM TAT SAT OM ☆☆☆

100

MESSAGES FROM THE TOTAPALLI HERMITAGE

On leaving my hermitage, what did it give to me?
Its firmness and noble strength, sweetness of its flowers,
And the Light of the Sun, dispelling all clouds.
Now, let me share this Light with you at all hours.

At the very thought of leaving Totapalli Hills, O! I felt the pangs of separation. As soon as I woke up on the last day of leaving Totapalli, I went down with the near and dear ones of the Ashram, to the foot of the hill and there, we had music and meditation, watching the rising Sun.

That day the question has been: What should I take from Totapalli Hills into the world of activity? These three were the prominent thoughts.

1) Let me take the firmness, the strength, of the Totapalli Hills.
2) Let me take the sweetness and forbearance of the sweet-smelling flowers, noting how they spread their fragrance though they are crushed under the very feet.
3) Let me take the Light of the Sun, into the world of activity and thus dispel all clouds of darkness. Let me share only the Effulgent Light with one and all!

Now, I am going forth into the world of activity and restlessness as Light of lights, filling the people as well as place with light, the Infinite and Eternal Light!

☆☆☆ OM TAT SAT OM ☆☆☆

101

FACE THE GOD EVEN IN THE UGLY

Face God everywhere, even in the ugly.
Don't see Him only in the beautiful, the best.
See Him in your foes, in the crooked and wicked.
To do so, to learn it, is the God-given test.

He alone can live as he pleases who sees the entire Universe as God or Himself. Freedom belongs to those who face God, the Reality even in the ugly and the so-called or mis-called foes. It is easy to see God in the best, the highest and the beautiful and in those who love and adore us. But how to see God, in the ugly, in the crooked and wicked and in those who misuse our love and hospitality and whose one purpose of life is to scheme, to hurt and wound us.

This is the God-given test, to know your present state and to overcome all weakness and fear. Hence, practise to see God in one and all and then you can live as you please, in all Peace and Freedom.

☆☆☆ OM TAT SAT OM ☆☆☆

102

WHO IS YOUR BEST FRIEND

Who sees the best in you, is your good friend.
He helps you to bring all things to a good end.
With him there is peace, there is power and poise,
You feel as God's child, and nothing annoys.

Who sees but the worst in you, is not your friend.
You feel bad and wicked, a burden to your land.
The worst that is in him, he sees in you too.
Recognize what is real, what is best, what is true.

He who sees the best in you is your good friend and he who brings out the Highest in you is your best friend.

There are some people in whose company we feel that we are mere crawling worms, the worst people, and a mere burden to mother earth. They see the worst in us and they bring out the worst from us, for they have the same thing in them. Like attracts like. What you have within, you behold the same in others or outside.

Again, there are people in whose company we feel Peace, Poise and Power. They help us to bring out the best and highest in us. They make us feel that we are the living Gods, knowing the best and highest, for we are the children of Immortality. May we recognize, the Real, the Best and the Highest Now and at all times!

☆☆☆ OM TAT SAT OM ☆☆☆

103

KEEP THE UPPER HAND IN DOING GOOD

Keep the upper hand in what you say,
Keep the upper hand in the right way.
It must be the truth, it must not be wrong.
In doing good always you will be strong.

Perhaps it is in Swamy Ram's works, we read that Johnson was the Prince of talkers. No one can beat him in arguments. He should have always the upper hand in any condition. It has been said of him; that if he misses the aim when he longs to shoot a person, he will beat him to death with the butt end of his pistol. It is wonderful to have such zeal and enthusiasm. But in many a case it is wrongly expressed and misused. There are many people who knowing that they are wrong, long to support their wrong or weak point and to prove what they say is right, regardless of the pain and suffering they cause to the innocent.

If they miss their aim to hurt you in one way, they will try a hundred other methods to condemn and crucify you, for they wish to have the upper hand in what they say, even though they themselves know that they are entirely wrong. May God bless them with the right vision!

☆☆☆ OM TAT SAT OM ☆☆☆

104

THE PATH OF TRUTH IS RUGGED

Blessed are they that choose the right path,
Though it is rugged, stay smiling and laugh.
Do not complain, for God is with you;
Bear the sorrows of the weak and the erring too.

The Path of Truth is very trying. It is uphill work. The weak, the weary and the faint-hearted can never tread it, for it is full of sharp stones and piercing thorns. The truth-seeker must crucify his little self before he begins to walk in the path of truth. Crucifixion from outside is nothing when compared to the death-like mental struggle, the inner crucifixion.

Blessed are they in whom the little self is dead! They alone can bear and suffer anything and everything silently without murmuring and grumbling. They do not complain, for all is God to them. Their one motto is: *Let no one suffer on my account. Let me suffer and suffer instead of others, bearing the sorrows of the weak and erring in the world of duality!*

☆☆☆ OM TAT SAT OM ☆☆☆

105

STORY OF THE BLEEDING FROG

A frog was hurt by Lord Rama's spear,
He had not seen that a frog was there.
O poor little frog, why did you not cry?
Why did you not call on me or give a sigh?

O Lord, said the frog, so I should do,
If others wound me; I should call then off you.
But when you yourself are hurting me,
Who else is there to see me free?

It is a little story. But what a deep meaning it has! It happened in the days of *Lord Sri Rama*, when he was leading a hermit's life in the forest. Once after a long roaming, he reached a marshy place and thrust his spear into the ground, since he wanted to rest there for a little while, with his dear ones, *Seeta* and *Lakshmana*.

After the needed rest, before leaving the place, Rama took out the spear that was thrust into the wet ground and was astonished to see blood at the end of it. When he examined the ground he saw to his sorrow a bleeding frog pierced by his spear to its very heart. Then the Lord said: "O, little unfortunate frog! Why did you not cry or make some sound when I was piercing you?" The little frog replied, "O Lord! When others hurt or wound me, I call on you seeking your help, but, when you yourself are spearing and hurting me to whom can I complain? Who else is there, for me to help and protect?" What a wise and touching answer!

May the Lord bless us with the wisdom, the fortitude and the forbearance of the little frog!

THE UNIVERSAL ANTHEM

One Cosmic Brotherhood,
One Universal Good
One Source, One Sway,
One Law beholding us,
One Purpose moulding us,
One Life enfolding us,
In Love Always.

☆ ☆ ☆

Anger, Resentment, Hate,
Long made us desolate,
Their Reign is done,
Race, Color, Creed and Caste,
Fade in the dreamy past
Man wakes to learn at last,
All Life is One!
Om! Om! Om!

☆☆☆ OM TAT SAT OM ☆☆☆

106

WHAT IS IT YOU WANT

What is it you want, to get or to do?
You have always desires, fresh and anew.
If you know yourself, all wishes disappear.
Be complete in yourself, and you've nothing to fear.

Be complete in yourself, get rid of this fire,
Driving you onward to new desire.
Who that has risen above want of every kind,
He only gets peace in his heart and his mind.

What is it you want, my child? Do you want to go to Mt. Kailas? Do you wish to go to the Himalayas? Do you wish to go to America? Where else do you want to go? What do you want to get? What else do you want to do? You want to do everything in the world except knowing Yourself.

When you know Yourself, all your wants and wishes disappear, for you are in Kailas, the Himalayas, in the U.S.A. and everywhere. As *self, the indivisible truth*, where is that place, where you do not exist already? As Self you have nothing to do and you are free of every want, for You are complete in yourself.

As such, all you need is only to get rid of this delusion of "want." Peace belongs to those who have risen above want of every kind.

☆☆☆ OM TAT SAT OM ☆☆☆

107

YOU ARE THE FRIEND OF YOURSELF

You need no one that is praising you,
You need none seeing but evil in you,
Who knows your faults best and what you've within?
Yourself is your best friend, who knows everything.

If you wish to realize the summum bonum of life, if you want to reach the very Heights get some one who loves you, and desires your spiritual welfare. You do not need the one, who flatters and praises you. You need some one who can tell you your faults, the blemishes within, so that you can be face to face with God, the Indwelling Light, rising above the passing clouds, which are covering the Sun of your life.

You do not need also anyone who over-does the fault finding only, sees evil in you, for what he sees in you is what is in him in the first place. He alone is the best friend, who can tell our faults but not he who flatters and praises to our face.

Hence, where is that best friend? However good and honest your friend may be, he is not expected to know all your faults. How can he know what you have within? Hence, one who knows your faults, your inner thoughts is not outside, but he is inside. He is yourself — YOU.

☆☆☆ OM TAT SAT OM ☆☆☆

108

SOMEBODY

Live an ideal life
For the one who loves you.
Don't disappoint the one,
Who always adores you.

To him you are all-in-all,
To him you are the life.
Be always his friend in need,
In luck and in strife.

Somebody loves you. Even if you are the poorest man, the most insignificant man in the world, you too have some one or other who loves and adores you. To that Somebody you are the life, soul, goal and all-in-all. That somebody may be your wife, child, father, mother, daughter or a friend to whom you are the all-in-all.

Is it not your bounden duty, to be true to that somebody, to live such an ideal life, that you will not disappoint that somebody, who loves and lives for you, considering you as his or her ideal? Here is a little poem on Somebody written by Somebody in the far away America, which is complete in itself, to express the essence of this message.

☆☆☆ OM TAT SAT OM ☆☆☆

SOMEBODY

Somebody did a golden deed,
Somebody proved a friend in need,
Somebody sang a beautiful song,
Somebody sailed the whole day long,
Somebody thought, "It's sweet to live";
Somebody said, "I am glad to give";
Somebody fought a valiant fight;
Somebody lived to shield the right;
Was that Somebody YOU?

☆☆☆ OM TAT SAT OM ☆☆☆

GLOSSARY

1. *Santhoyam Atma.*	The Atma ever rests in Peace.
2. *Ekameva Advithiyam.*	The Real is One without a Second.
3. *Brahman.*	The Absolute.
4. *Satchitananda.*	Pure Existence, Knowledge and Bliss.
5. *Sat eva Somya idam asith agre.*	O my good son! the Real was alone present in the beginning.
6. *Yogas Chitta Vritti nirodha.*	Cessation of the modifications of the mind is Yoga.
7. *Bhauman.*	Boundless.
8. *Brihat.*	Great.
9. *Atmana Kamaya.*	Desire Through Self.
10. *Satva-Rajas-Tamas.*	(literal meaning is) Existence, activity, and darkness
11. *Karmani Akarmayah Pasyeth Akarmanicha Karmayaha.*	See action in inaction and inaction in action.
12. *Karmadyaksha.*	Master of all works.
13. *Thasya bhasaa Sarvamidam Vibhathi.*	The whole world shines by His illumination.
14. *Pasya-me-yogam-aisvaram.*	Behold my Divine Power of Yoga.
15. *Samadhi.*	God consciousness.
16. *Sutreh mani gana.*	Like precious gems threaded on a string.
17. *Poornamadaha-Poornam-idam-*	That (*Brahman*) is Infinite. This (world) is Infinite. Even when this

Poornath Poornam-udhachyathe Poornasya Poornamadhaya Poornameva Avasishyathe.	comes from that That alone remains.
18. *Soham.*	I am that Brahman.
19. *Sahaja Samadhi.*	Constant abidance in God. Consciousness.
20. *Ashtavakra Gita.*	The Gita by Sage Ashtavakra.
21. *Anando Brahma.*	Brahman is Blissful.
22. *Prana.*	Breath
23. *Nathasya Karyam Karanam cha Vidyathe.*	There is nothing more to be done or left undone.
24. *Videha Kaivalya.*	While Still in the world Liberated.
25. *Maya.*	Illusion.
26. *Atman.*	Self.

☆ ☆ ☆ OM TAT SAT OM ☆ ☆ ☆

SELECT IMPRESSIONS OF THE READERS OF THE COSMIC FLASHES IN THE EAST AND THE WEST

1. "My heartiest congratulations for '*Cosmic Flashes*'. It is more than wonderful, nay it is your very Soul that you are giving! Sending my impressions in the form of *Verses*. Now once more I assure you my joy and greatest appreciation with my heartiest thanks for the precious gift of your *Cosmic Flashes*".

Irmgard Georga Schultz. — Germany. (Ganga Mayi)

2. "Like the 40 days fast of Jesus Christ, Swami Omkar of Santi Ashram, Totapalli Hills, East Godavari District, South India, underwent a similar fast in March–April 1950 and the thought-waves or *Cosmic Flashes* of those days have been caught by the pen of Omkarji and condensed in this lovely book. It contains lofty thoughts. A perusal of any chapter gives passivity to the active mind. Swamiji's sublime thoughts in the form of *Cosmic Flashes* are there for all times as the 108 petals of a heavenly flower. The publishers have no copyright, so anyone is at liberty to reprint a portion or the whole book. Swami Omkar will be pleased to present a copy of the *Cosmic Flashes* to any Seeker of Truth".

M. Chinniah, Kuala Lumpur

3. "Glad to hear from you again. *Cosmic flashes* arrived yesterday. You will be surprised to hear that the book contains just what I have been praying for all these years. It has given me light on the path." *Horace A. Cronk. St. Paul — U.S.A.*

4. "*Cosmic Flashes* is a good book. The messages are good and inspiring and the get up is also very good. May it bring light and comfort to our brethren."

M. Ruttonjee & Son Ltd — Hongkong

5. "*Cosmic Flashes* is immensely good. I can walk along the path as almost all the selections are very apt. I, myself, have had so many of these flashes, that I find in Swami Omkarji a kindred soul indeed, though I doubt not that He has risen much higher than me in this earthly life."

Mrs. Phillippa Merry Mansur — California, U.S.A.

6. "It is the first book in my life, that has such a wonderful introduction. We must translate your *Cosmic Flashes* into German. My way lies with your way. I found also in your book introduction by your bosom-friend Satchidananda Murty."

Albert Moldenhauer — Husum (Germany)

7. "*Cosmic Flashes* came into my hands. It was received on the eve of my birthday! Many teachings have come into my hands for the past few years, in which I have been seeking Reality. *Cosmic Flashes* appealed to me and has become useful in my morning devotions."

Dr. Don. C. Hatt — Toronto, Canada

8. "By the grace of thy loving kindness my dear wife and myself received the copies of thy wonderful work *Cosmic Flashes*. From this book we do read daily and feel the close attunement of the Divine Presence within and with thee. Often do I visit thee and feel the Divine Vibrations of thy presence."

Dr. & Mrs. Preston Kline Caye — Los Angeles 14

9. "I am grateful to you for sending me a copy of *Cosmic Flashes*. It was great delight to go through the book, so simple and yet so great. The 108 prayers are like the beads of a complete wreath used for the purpose of a Japa as with each page, there is complete remembrance of God."

Sri H.B. Parikh, Bombay

10. "I thank you very much for the Calico-bound copy of *Cosmic Flashes*. I have just finished reading. As I have said in the introduction it is so wonderful. I understand *fully* and *highly* appreciate your desire not to advertise it and send for reviews. I am also glad that you do not wish to have its copies sold. That is the real spirit of a *Sannyasi*. A Sannyasi should have as his sole purpose the spreading of *Brahma-Vidya*, but he should not seek to make money out of it. It is the true spirit of the real *Parivrajaka*."

Dr. K. Satchidananda Murty, M.A,, Ph.D., — Waltair

11. "I thank you for the copy of Cosmic Flashes kindly sent to me. Your thoughts are, as usual, elevating. I am sure that those who happen to read the Flashes will be immensely benefited."

Dr. T.M.P. Mahadavan, M.A., Ph.D., — Madras

12. "We accept with joy and gratitude your presentation copy of "*Cosmic Flashes*". It is inspiring and wonderful.

Sri Swami Ramdas. Anandasram, Kanjangad

13. "The Cosmic Flashes" sent by you is more than excellent. Its merit can be realised only by those in the line.

K.S. Venkatraman M.A., I.C.S., Distt. Judge, Tanjore

14. "It is with deep gratitude that I accept your very beautiful present of the *Cosmic Flashes*. I am happy to tell you that my home circle read it in the quiet of the night, and we have found it most inspiring. We are sometimes transported to sublime heights, reading the beautiful thoughts in it. It is our fervent hope and prayer that some day we shall have the fortune to visit your Ashram and receive your blessings".

Sri D.C. Wiratunga — Proctor, Ceylon

15. "At this particular moment, my mind is concentrated on your most loving book, *Cosmic Flashes*, which our beloved friend Sri Doraswami has sent to me for perusal. It is a mine of deep, Divine thoughts, tingling with that splendour, which can emanate only from a heart that is in tune with the Infinite, a mind that is soaked in God, a soul that is enrapport with the Eternal.

I salute the Christ Spirit, the Krishna Spirit, the Jorast Spirit that is in you. People are so lost in Maya, that they cannot realize this fact, that knowledge of the Self alone can break all barriers to Bliss Eternal. You fasted for forty days in silence and gave yourself up entirely to prayers and meditations. It was not fasting. You were feasting with God. Am I right? I have enjoyed your book, thoroughly.

Sri M.K. Spencer, Karachi